IMPROVE YOUR POSITION

MICHAEL ALEXANDER

CONTENTS

DEDICATION

This book is dedicated to my family and to each one who has caused or supported this change in me. I am grateful.

To everyone who thinks that struggle and losing is their identity, it's not true.

To every human being going through something they prefer to keep to themselves.

This is for you!

TESTIMONIALS

There are a lot of lessons to be learned and much inspiration to be had examining the life of Mike Alexander. From a very humble beginning to a human that's seen and done more than most ever dare imagine. His story will motivate you.

— SEAN SHELBY, UFC MATCHMAKER

"Intestinal fortitude, grit, and perseverance. All core pillars you will be invigorated with once finishing this book. Mike's a warrior, survivor, motivator, and authentic human being that isn't afraid to open his heart to the world so the world can become a better place."

— DR. GINO COLLURA BEHAVIORAL SCIENTIST

Michael Alexander's book, "Improve Your Position," reminds me very much of the principles of success in martial arts. I've been training for close to twenty years and two concepts have always stood above all, consistency and discipline. This story consists of hard work and a disciplined mindset. No matter how challenging the situation, you can still be a guiding light to any who are lost. I recommend this truly inspirational book to anyone for a strong, grounded dose of reality. Read this book and you'll be motivated and taught how to improve your position in life.

— ALEX MORONO, UFC FIGHTER

Michael Alexander left a lasting impression on Springtown ISD. His awesome talent in football and track were only exceeded by his honesty, character, and integrity. Most times in high school, I strive as a coach to help my players become better people, something I do through relationships. Well, Michael made me a better person through our relationship. His book, Improve Your Position will make you a better person also.

— COACH GARY RUSHING HIGH SCHOOL
FOOTBALL AND TRACK COACH

Michael Alexander has consistently demonstrated throughout his life that adversity is nothing more than a character building opportunity. No matter what life has dealt him, he's found a way to improve his position. As a result, you can see why he's so revered and respected in the BJJ and MMA communities. I'm grateful to call him a friend and client. This book is a must-read for anyone needing a dose of motivation.

— JASON HOUSE CVO – IRIDIUM SPORTS
AGENCY

FOREWORD

I'm happy for you because you have this book. Although it's mainly about the amazing true story of my friend, Mike, you're about to receive an infusion of inspiration. From the outside looking in, one could say that life was cruel to Mike; it's almost as if he was constantly dealt a bad hand. Yet, as you'll discover, a few bad hands can't hold back a fighter. Mike is a fighter, always has been, always will be.

I first met Mike through my younger brother, Paul. They attended the same elementary and middle school and were very close friends. Being that Mike lived just three streets away, Mike became a fourth brother to us. When his younger brother was born, he was at our house. New Year's Eve, he was at our house running down the street banging pots and pans. Pretty much every weekend, Mike was at our house playing whiffle ball, football, and anything else we could play or invent to compete against each other. The first thing I noticed was that Mike was freakishly athletic. The second thing I noticed was that he was crazy-competitive, just like me. From backyard games to challenging other kids to play football and baseball, we all knew with Mike on our team, we had a damn good chance to win.

I often recall the many times we went at it. Even though the memories are fond, they were vicious. One time, we got into a heated argument that turned into a full-on fistfight over whether someone was safe or not on first base during a whiffle ball game. Another time, in the heat of debating the pointless topics of backyard sports, I threw a lawn chair at him and started another scuffle.

Although Mike and I fought a bit growing up, it was always in the heat of sport – we fought like brothers, not enemies. We fought like warriors. From an early age, we fought to win. That fight is still there, but now it is to win at life.

I look around and see many people with a candle burning inside them. A passion and desire to be better, a fire for competition. Mike doesn't have that candle; he has a forest fire in him, which is a rarity. Not just to win in sports but also in the higher-stakes game of life. He fought through serious adversity during his childhood. Growing up in a blue-collar neighborhood, he was not afforded any head starts in life and had to fight every step of the way. He fought his way through legal issues that would cripple most people. He fought his way to an invitation to the NFL Combine. He started in construction and fought his way up the ranks to be a renowned and respected COO and high-level executive who helped build Globe Life Field (Texas Rangers Stadium) and other multi-million dollar projects and hospitals. He fought in MMA before transitioning to Jiu-Jitsu, where he is now a two-time World Champion. In every phase of his life, Mike has fought and improved his position.

Life happens, Mike moved to another city and went to another high school. It's fair to say that during college and the years after, we lost touch, sometimes not talking for months or years. We had a very loose association, primarily through social media, until one day, he called me out of the blue.

I had gotten a job with UFC in 2013 and moved from Los Angeles to Las Vegas. Around that time, Mike was training his ass off in Jiu-Jitsu. He called to congratulate me on the new job. He had no motive, and his simple, thoughtful action got us reconnected. As Mike continued to fight, I did as well, doing everything I could to learn the UFC business and add value to the company. UFC is an amazing institution, and I have been afforded the opportunity to contribute in various roles --even working often and directly with the big man himself, Dana White. I was eventually given the opportunity to lead the non-UFC live events division on UFC Fight Pass. These are all the organizations you fight in to get signed to the UFC.

It was great to reconnect with Mike, and when I had the chance, I would bring him to a UFC event or watch him compete in BJJ. In one of the many conversations we had watching a fight, he told me that he had done a little commentating with some small shows and asked for a shot to commentate with Fury FC, an organization based in Houston.

This question was a pivotal moment, and to understand that, you have to know a little about me: I'm also a fighter – not a competitive fighter, but I hate to lose. I am not willing to risk my reputation on people I don't trust to come through, regardless of relationship or hometown roots. To say this was a big favor is an understatement. But this was Mike, and I knew he was the type of guy you bet on.

I texted Eric Garcia, the owner of Fury FC, and told him about Mike, a long-time friend, BJJ world champion, and hard worker. I asked him one question: "Can you give him a shot?" I knew Mike was a winner, and Eric could see that he was - so he gave him a shot.

Mike got his chance, not as a primetime commentator, but with a few non-broadcast prelim bouts. Mike did what he's always done: he seized the moment and improved his position from off-broadcast to main card prime time. He now has one of the most viewed post-fight interviews on YouTube.

Now, as you are about to embark on his story, I believe you will come away inspired. You'll see that no situation is ever too bad if you're willing to fight to improve your position. It may take a day, a week, or even years, but if you're consistent and willing to fight, like Mike, you'll turn life's bad hands into inspirational stories.

Stephen Tecci
Vice President, PPV and UFC Fight Pass

1

SHUT UP AND PERFORM

IT'S ABOUT PERFORMANCE

WHAT YOU READ IN THE FOLLOWING FEW LINES MIGHT COME across as harsh, just please understand that I don't intend to be. The reason I start my book this way is so that we find common ground as people. Ready? Here it is. With love...

No one really cares about what you've been through.

If you've been through crazy, traumatic, heart-breaking things in life, like me, you may have told people what happened to you, and if those people cared for you, you probably got the reaction you desired.

"What?"

"No way!"

"Oh, poor you!"

"How do you deal with that?"

"I'm so sorry that happened to you."

It may have felt good because it's the reaction you hoped for. As human beings, we tend to continue to do things that feel good, hence why there are so many alcoholics - they like to drink, or how the alcohol makes them feel, so they continue even when it starts to destroy parts or all of their lives. Unfortunately for alcoholics and anyone with an unhealthy addiction, even when they succumb to their guilty pleasure of choice – overeating, fast food, binge-watching, weed, prescription drugs, illegal drugs, social media, phones, or toxic relationships – they continue to do it. This is why bars are still packed, the Taco Bell drive-thru is still busy at 3 AM, and people start streaming Season 7 of a show even though it's way past their bedtime and they have to wake up early the next day.

In the same way, people who have had unfortunate or catastrophic pasts keep telling others what happened to them. The problem is, as unhealthy addictions hurt us in the long run, so does constantly replaying or crying about the past. Look, you can only tell people what happened to you for so

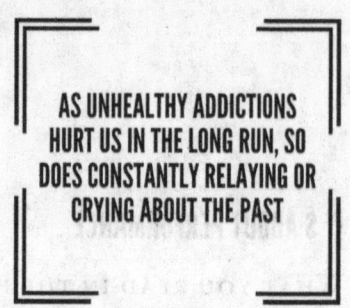

AS UNHEALTHY ADDICTIONS HURT US IN THE LONG RUN, SO DOES CONSTANTLY RELAYING OR CRYING ABOUT THE PAST

long before they expect you to do what you're supposed to and don't want to hear any more excuses. Millions of people today, maybe billions, are addicted to getting sympathy. The woe-is-me addiction is as real as any other. Just like any other, it has adverse side effects.

FREE YOURSELF

I hate to break it to you, but people don't care as much as you think they do. Let me put it this way: a new bartender who was raped when she was nine years old starts working at a swanky bar. (I bring up this analogy because it's one of the worst I can think of). A man that looks like her abuser walks in and she freaks out. She starts to hyperventilate and has a full-blown panic attack. The manager and owner rush to her and find out why she reacted that way. They understand. They tell her to rest in the manager's office or take the rest of the day off – as any decent human being, I think, would do.

Three days later, she comes to work, and the same thing happens. She tells them, again, why she's reacting that way. Again, they understand. Maybe they let her go home... again. The real-world question is, how long do you think she can do that and keep her job?

Suppose you're the owner or manager, and it happened five times out of her first fifteen days of work. In that case, that's five times they are understaffed or had to call in other people who thought they had the day off and made other plans to come in to work and help them get out of a jam. In the meantime, first-time patrons receive terrible service so they'll never go there again. Would you let her go or would you allow the reputation of the bar and your relationship with every other bartender to become handicapped because of what happened to your new bartender when she was nine?

Too many people use their horrific pasts as excuses for them not to be held accountable or as accountable as others. I'm sensitive to every form of trauma you may have been through, and I'll agree that it sucks – wait till you read MY story – but the truth remains, people just don't care all that much.

If you can be objectively honest, you most likely know people that have been through tough times. How often do you think about it or them? You probably love someone a great deal that went through hell, but you don't call the person every day, send Christmas and birthday presents every year. It's not that you're an insensitive asshole – it's just a fact that people don't care as much for others' pasts as some think they do.

> IF YOU DEPEND ON SYMPATHY, ALLOWANCES FOR POOR PERFORMANCE, AND GUILT-ING PEOPLE INTO GIVING YOU CHANCE AFTER CHANCE, YOU'LL LIVE A MISERABLE LIFE.

I say this to help you free yourself – your problems, past, and demons are yours to deal with. If you depend on sympathy, allowances for poor performance, and guilt-ing people into giving you chance after chance, you'll live a miserable life. Probably more miserable than the one you gripe about because the thing that happened to you in your past happened when you may have been a child, when you had no choice or power, but the life you create now, as an adult, is 100% because of your choices. <u>Dear reader and new friend, the only thing that matters from here on out is how you perform.</u>

Too many have leaned on their excuses for so long it's become part of their identity. I want you to understand that if you've been through hell, it's over. You've been through it. If you're going through hell, that's different, you're going through it, but if it's behind you, there's no need to go back to it or

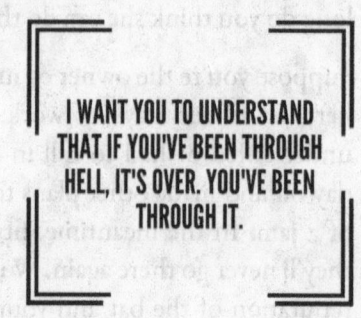

I WANT YOU TO UNDERSTAND THAT IF YOU'VE BEEN THROUGH HELL, IT'S OVER. YOU'VE BEEN THROUGH IT.

let it define you. You're a survivor. You're a bad ass. You've walked through puddles others would have drowned in. It's not time to complain again. It's time to compete. It's time to win.

THIS THING CALLED LIFE

I'm not downplaying or minimizing the horrible things people do to each other or unfortunate events. Maybe you were physically, mentally, or emotionally abused as a child. Maybe your peers, educators, or people in authority over you shunned you. Maybe you loved someone, a parent, spouse, child, cousin, aunt, uncle, or best friend, and they committed suicide. Maybe something outside your control derailed your career plans, health, or financial status. Perhaps because of something that happened to you, you're afraid of the dark, the ocean, being in crowds, attention, spiders, clowns, or the supernatural world. Maybe at one time, you felt you had limitless potential – either you thought it or others told you – but you've landed far short of where you thought you would. Maybe you thought you'd have done more in your life than you have. Perhaps you've seen others with fewer skills than you zoom past you. Maybe you see people living the life you always felt you were destined for.

Chances are, you've gone through bad, sad, emotionally horrific, painful experiences. Maybe, like me, you've cried until you thought you had run out of tears, only to experience freshly-created hot tears streaming down your face with greater velocity than before. Maybe, like me, you've felt that you screwed yourself repeatedly. Perhaps, like me, you've blown once-in-a-lifetime opportunities you'd never get back. Maybe, like me, you're the bad guy in other people's stories.

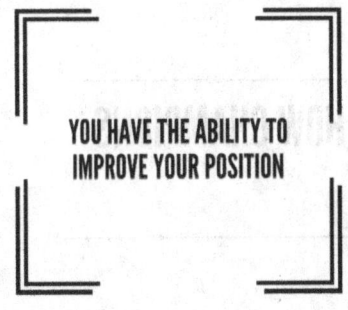

YOU HAVE THE ABILITY TO IMPROVE YOUR POSITION

If you can relate to any of that, welcome to this thing called life; a journey filled with beauty and terror. What happened before you read this book already happened. Regardless of how hard you try, you can't change it. What is in your power, though, and I hope you like this – is that you have the ability to improve your position. If you can improve your position a little every day, you'll live a much better life.

Contained in this book are answers you may have no idea you've been searching for. As you read my story – the good, the bad, and the ugly – and see how I went from being nearly murdered multiple times as a child to going to prison to a becoming a Jiu Jitsu World Champion, high level executive/entrepreneur, actor, and broadcaster on UFC Fight Pass, take heart that you can change the trajectory of your life as well. As you uncover the many life lessons I've been blessed or forced to learn, you'll realize an amazing truth: the good ole' days are now!

2

GETTING YOUR ASS KICKED: HOW CHAMPIONS ARE MADE

JIU-JITSU WORLD CHAMPIONSHIP

IT WAS LIKE THE KARATE KID MOVIE, THE FIRST ONE, NOT the twelve crappy ones that followed. The gymnasium was packed. The IBJJF (International Brazilian Jiu-Jitsu Federation) Purple Belt No Gi World Championship was on the line. Excitement was in the air. And I was injured just like Daniel LaRusso's character, aka Danielsan.

I was at the Walter Pyramid, a 4,000-seat, indoor multi-purpose arena on the Long Beach State University campus in Long Beach, California. I was competing for the second time in the World IBJJF No Gi Jiu-Jitsu Championship (International Brazilian Jiu-Jitsu Federation). When I left my home in Texas, flying out of DFW (the Dallas-Fort Worth Airport), I knew in my bones I would win. My confidence did not come from competing the previous year because I lost in the very first round; instead, it came from knowing I had prepared myself to the fullest; I had not cut corners, I had learned, I had pushed myself more than ever before, and I just felt that if I ever did that, I'd be unstoppable. And I was a GREAT student.

Like most fighters, I have a ritual on fight day. While some go to bed or wake up at a specific time, and others make sure to eat a particular food or talk to a certain person, I don't rest. I'm not the guy that Zen's out, reflecting or meditating. Not on fight day, I'm too restless. So that morning, my wife and I went to the nearby Aquarium of the Pacific and took a stroll, admiring the many sights instead of planning for the challenge ahead. I needed to occupy my mind with something besides the task at hand. I couldn't afford to overthink it, we arrived an hour and a half before my first match.

I went right to the warm-up room. Another ritual I have is I don't watch other people's matches before mine. Fighting is, after all, the most brutal of all sports. I don't like watching other people getting hurt, and I don't like the emotions of watching people win, or lose. It throws off my mental rhythm. I stayed in the back, getting my body loose and my mind ready until my name was called. It was time for all my work to pay off. Being that I was a relative no-name compared to some of the other fighters, I don't think I got a roar from the crowd when the referee called for us to enter the mat. I didn't care either way, I was dialed in. The only thing in my head was, *be strong, be fast, be strong, be fast...*

I knew my opponent, although I'm unsure if he knew me. After all, as I mentioned, I did lose my first match the previous year. However, I felt I could overpower him. Unlike MMA and boxing matches, there are no rounds in Brazilian Jiu-Jitsu tournaments. It's one brutal 7-minute match at a time against everyone in your bracket. To put that in perspective, boxing is three minutes and MMA rounds are five minutes.

The match began and when we clashed the first time: I was right, I could overpower him. I took him down and had a dominant position on him after several scrambles. I got him in a D'Arce choke, my favorite finishing move, and submitted him. For the fighting-impaired who may not know what a D'Arce choke is, I wrapped my arms around his neck with his topside arm in and squeezed until he quit by tapping out. It took all of 90 seconds for me to do much better than I did the previous year! Round 1 of the bracket was complete. I was moving to the next round.

Unfortunately for me, my next opponent was favored to win the entire tournament. His name is Luc Bondole. At the time, he was undefeated in MMA (2-0) and fought for Bellator, one of the biggest fight promotions in the world. The dude was scary. The weight limit was 202 lbs., but Luc must have walked around at around 220-225 lbs., meaning he had to cut weight to make a weight I couldn't even get to. They listed him at 6'2 but I never believed it, the man was a giant.

Unlike the previous match, when we clashed the first time, I didn't think I could overpower him, yet, I also felt strong and didn't think he could bully me either. We wrestled on our feet using all our strength, trying to find an opening or advantage for a takedown. We were in a clinch, and I used all my strength to make him go backward when I felt a pop in my knee. I knew right there I had severed or torn my meniscus. I lost all my power to take him down.

There was only one way I could win: baiting him to take me down, which was a terrifying thought because of how big, strong, and skilled he was. We clinched again and I orchestrated his takedown of me so that as soon as we hit the mat, I could scramble to get into position. Unfortunately, he was also fast and stuffed me. I was down 4-0 on points and time was expiring. All he had to do was smother me for two more minutes and he'd secure the win.

I managed to get a little distance from him and scrambled as hard as possible and improved my position. After the scramble, my hands were on his head, trying to snake their way around his neck. I created another scramble with a short burst of going to his right. When he moved with me, I countered and my hands were at his neck. I had it. A Japanese Necktie! I squeezed with every fiber of my being. Then I felt one of the best feelings ever in my life. Luc friggin Bondole tapped on my knee. I had beaten the odds-on favorite!

There was one match to go for the Brazilian Jiu-Jitsu World Championship. However, instead of being excited or celebrating the upset win, I thought, *Oh crap! I'm fucking injured!*

HAWAIIAN BORN, BUT FAR FROM PARADISE!

I certainly did not have a fairytale upbringing. I was born in Hawaii but moved when I was a baby, so I have no recollection of it. My father was in the Army and my mother was addicted to drugs. She left him and took us all – my older brother and younger sister – to Texas. My earliest memory would be indicative of how the next few years would be for us. Thankfully, Jason, my older brother, helped clear up the foggy memories of our crazy upbringing.

My brother and I were sitting on the floor, watching TV at around 2 AM. The house was full of people walking in and out as always. Suddenly, the door busted open and shouts and lights overtook the room. The SWAT team was raiding our house!

A female officer grabbed me, brought me behind the sofa, and covered me with her body, putting me between her hands and knees.

"Shhhhh, please, sit still. Everything is going to be okay. No one is going to get hurt."

What she could never comprehend was that I wasn't scared. I was happy they were there! Although I was a kid, I was already sick and tired of people coming in and out of the house every hour of the day or night. I didn't know much about the world but knew that my mother was doing bad things (I didn't know the term illegal). And that, my friend, is my first memory of being alive.

At the time, I had no idea how to know what had happened, but they did arrest her and take her away. I'd be lying if I wrote that I wished they had locked her up forever and I was sent to a new family, but although that might be true, I don't remember anything else of that night. What I do know is that she came home the next day. It never dawned on me that perhaps she had rolled over and told on (ratted out) who she got the drugs from or worked with. All I knew was that she was back home. That sucked.

Before you judge me for my feelings for my mother, please understand that I don't have one good memory of her. Although, at times, she'd be nurturing and loving to my brother and sister, she was never like that with me. At times she'd beat me so bad that when I was in kindergarten, first grade, or second grade, I had to be absent, probably so child services wouldn't come snooping around. In lieu of hugs and kisses, I got loose teeth, a busted lip, black eyes, and a lifetime's worth of curses.

I'm not saying I was an angel as a kid. I was a live wire. I was very inquisitive, always asking questions, which at times to her, perhaps, came across as questioning her decision-making or authority. I couldn't sit still for too long and quickly got bored of everything. My brother could watch a two-hour movie but 30 minutes in, I'd want to play catch or run outside. Still, the price for being rambunctious should not have been beatings and berating's. It certainly didn't warrant being murdered!

TO BE OR NOT TO BE

A few months before the SWAT raid, my brother and I were taking a bath. My mother had yelled at us several times already to hurry up. When she walked into the bathroom, she saw me laughing, splashing my brother – no doubt making a nice little wet mess on the bathroom floor.

She handed my brother a towel and told him to go to the room to get dressed. I knew she was pissed so I hurriedly tried to get out of the tub also. She held me there until my brother left, and although I don't remember what she said, I can never forget the menacing look on her face as she said it. The next thing I knew, my head was under the water. Thankfully, my brother returned to the bathroom and saw her forcibly holding my head down while my little body squirmed as if I was being electrocuted, no doubt fighting to breathe. He ran to her and pushed her away from me. I quickly jumped out of the tub and ran to the room to hide under the covers, naked and soaking wet. Jason's heroic act saved my life. He told me later, as adults, that he cried for days after because he thought he would be in trouble for pushing her.

A few days after the SWAT raid, my brother and I watched TV in the living room at around 2 AM, which, as you can see, is common in a trap house. The difference was that we were the only people there, just our family, not the riff-raff that came to get high at our home. Suddenly, my mother ran into the room and turned off the TV and the lights. I don't recall any conversation, but shortly thereafter, there was a loud banging on the door.

I whispered to my mother, "Is that the police?"

She whispered back, "No. Just a dumb friend. Let's all be very still and quiet and he'll leave soon enough."

"Open the fucking door!" a voice shouted from outside the door. "I know you're there. Come on. We have to talk!"

So I'm sitting there, quiet in the dark, and her dumb friend continues to bang on the door. I was too young to understand that my mother was scared to death. All I knew was that I was beyond bored and aggravated.

"Don't make this worse! Open the door!"

I couldn't hold it. I yelled as loud as I could. "No one is home. Go away!"

My mother grabbed me by the neck and pushed me into my room. The door banging increased in tempo and volume, as did the shouts from outside the door.

I saw my mother run to her room and come out with a robe and slippers. She opened the door in mid-yawn, acting as if she was asleep and had been woken up. Mind you, I'm a kid, maybe in first grade – I saw hands roughly grab my mother and take her.

Whoever it was took her to the yard and beat the shit out of her. I thought I should go there and tell them to leave her alone. But I don't know if I knew exactly what was happening, and to be truthful, if maybe I wanted it to happen. She eventually came into the house bloody and crying. Putting the pieces together as adults, my brother and I believe whoever she ratted out to get out of jail from the raid had come to *pay her a visit.*

The very next day, she drew a bath and called me to the bathroom. I went there, fully clothed, because that's what you do when your mom calls you, you go to her. She told me to come close, and when I did, she grabbed me and tried to drown me again. I was fighting and kicking not to become submerged and managed to let out a scream or two. I can vividly remember being under the water, seeing her as she struggled to keep me there. That memory should be unclear, I actually wish I could forget it, but it's still as clear as day to me.

Again, Jason came to the rescue. "Leave him alone, mom. You're going to go to jail!"

He managed to get me away from her, although I left crying, barely able to breathe, and with deep fingernail marks on my face and neck.

That was the second time my mother tried to murder me!

3

EVERYONE CAN COME EXCEPT FOR MICHAEL

DON'T INTERACT WITH YOUR MOTHER

THE EARLY YEARS OF MY LIFE WERE FILLED WITH dangerous, scandalous, unethical adults. As I think on it now, knowing there are horrible and evil people in the world, I actually consider myself lucky that I was never molested, abducted, or anything like that. My biggest problem was my mothers abusive, and sometimes murderous intentions, which was bad enough!

As a kid, it's easy to lose respect for adults you see get high as shit. They would come in the house smiling, coherent, talking, intelligently expressing themselves, etc., but then they'd go to a room and come out comatose and zombie-like. It became common sense for me not to give a shit what they said or thought. I certainly never took their words of advice as wisdom. Other times, some would come out of the room, coked up, talking about the stupidest shit, even for a kid. However, there was one guy who was dating my mother at the time that I did listen to.

He would constantly tell her she needed to stop beating me, treating me, talking to me, and talking about me the way she did. Maybe she did it more for him, but she made life a little easier for me by simply ignoring me. I learned that I could do whatever I wanted, including going outside at 1 or 2 in the morning, so long as I didn't interrupt her, which meant, I didn't even have to ask for permission.

He also told me I had to stop provoking her. "Look, little man, if you want your mom to stop fucking you up, you have to stop provoking her." That was the only voice of reason I had heard in my seven years of life. The advice was pretty much – *don't interact with your mother.* So, I tried not to. It was like I didn't have a parent.

MIKE, I AM YOUR FATHER

In a blink of an eye, my father joined the picture. Mind you, this all happened during an era before social media. My dad, being a military man and then a mason – a bricklayer, wasn't up to speed on technology. I don't know how he found us, but one day I avoided my mother and her druggie friends; the next day, my brother, sister, and I were living with my dad. My whole world changed and I could not have been happier.

My dad lived better than my mom, especially considering he wasn't a drug addict. He was a hard worker who barely drank and never did drugs. On the other hand, I was still the rambunctious kid who said whatever came to my mind, a trait that is a blessing for me now but was catastrophic during my childhood.

My father tried to teach me early on what he did for a living. It could have been more to show me a good work ethic, so kudos to him for it now. I knew I did not want to be like him when I grew up by seeing how hard he worked and realizing that we didn't have much to live on. Of course, I didn't just think it, I would tell him, repeatedly.

It didn't take long for me to discover that he believed in corporal punishment. He didn't beat me with a belt, he did it with a board. I went from being slapped by a woman occasionally to being hit just about every day with a board by a man.

I don't know why but I never stopped provoking him. I never changed. I'd challenge him all the time. It was like our thing; he'd warn me that he'd hit me if I didn't stop doing X. I'd tell him I didn't want to stop and keep doing it. He'd hit me, I'd hate my life, and we would do it again the next day and the next. To say I grew up defiant and with no fear would be an understatement.

I was like that everywhere, not just at home. I'm sure I was a terror as an elementary school student. I just always had so much energy. So much so that people didn't want me around. They'd tell my dad, "Jason and Joni can come, but not Michael." I had lived with my mother, and it fucking sucked, I then lived with my dad, and although there were no more attempted murders on my life, that also fucking sucked. Life just sucked all the way around.

DO IT YOURSELF OR IT WON'T HAPPEN

Now, dear reader, I'd like to address you specifically. Talk to you, if you will. The reason for this book is not to tell you my life's story, the goal of it is to lay it down as a foundation so that I can share some of the many lessons I've learned to become the person I am today.

There are going to be people that will tell you, you won't amount to much. I heard it just about every day. The adults in my life were primarily losers that hated themselves. People will tell you negative things so you can share in their misery; after all, misery loves company.

They don't think they deserve any better from life and don't think you should either. So, even though they may feel their advice comes from a place of love or for you not to get hurt, or you not to fail, or you not to be embarrassed, you have to understand they're not helping you, they're hurting you! Not just the you today but the better, happier you that you can be in the future.

I want to impress upon you that where you start or are now does not have to determine how you'll end up. You can realize this truth tomorrow, in twenty years, or when you're 72 and have nothing but bad memories and regrets. My advice? Be bold. Take risks. Make moves. If you don't like something about your life, change it. It is, after all, your life!

Too many people are scared to try to live better lives. They think they'll fail and go back to the bottom. I want to shake the shit out of those people and make them realize, "You're already at the bottom! Try to move up. If you fail, the bottom will be here waiting for you. Don't live your entire life without at least giving it a try!"

They get scared because they don't have the entire road map to their destination. Life isn't like that! No one has it all figured out. If you leave LA and drive to New York, you won't be able to see every inch of the road. At night, all you'll see is as far as your headlights show you. Too many people are paralyzed, waiting for "sure things" or "silver bullets" or a genie granting them three wishes, and live and die in LA, never being awed by the Grand Canyon in Arizona, never thrilled by the Great Smokey Mountains of Tennessee, and never experiencing the mass of humanity in Time Square or take in the breathtaking sight from atop the Statue of Liberty.

No matter your situation, someone was in a worse position and got out of it. No matter your upbringing, many people had a worse situation and did great things with their lives. There are world champions, billionaires, celebrities, and billions of people happy with their lives that came from worse. I'm not Tony Robbins, I'm not a motivational guru, but if you allow yourself to be open, I can tell you that nothing and no one but you is stopping you from living a better life.

You just read how my life started. I know many others who have had better upbringings but have become victims of their pasts. They didn't have it as tough as I did, but they accepted the lie that they weren't worth the trouble of fighting for more. While they were kids, meaning when they had little control over their lives, they accepted defeat for the rest of their lives. They've given up on themselves before they ever became adults!

I don't need Dr. Gino Collura or some therapist to tell me I hated myself growing up. I truly hated myself. I hated my mother. I hated my life. What's worse was that my self-loathing was validated because the adults hated me too. My subconscious thoughts were - *If they hate me, I must be hate-able.*

I'm no motivational guru, but I'll share what I did that derailed me from living a horrible life; even though I went to prison, a story I will share later in this book. I changed how I thought and spoke to myself. Your fears will come to your mind unbidden, we can't control them, but you can control what you say about yourself. I didn't know I'd become a freak athlete, but I did know I would live a better life than my father and mother. I had blind faith I was destined for better.

As you'll see as we continue with my life story, things didn't get better. One could argue that it got a little worse, but because I saw myself better, I found a tool that would help me for the rest of my life. I only found it, though, because I made a decision that life wouldn't break me. You may be at a point in time where you need to decide on who you want to be from this day forward.

Faith is a powerful thing. I'm not referring to it in a religious context, although that's powerful too. But faith in yourself, that you're worth more, that you can change for the better, that life happens for you and not to you, that you are unique and possess the ability and talents to live an extraordinary life – is incredibly powerful.

If an area of your life sucks, change it by changing your mind about what's possible. Change your mind by changing the losers you allow to hang around you. That may be your childhood friends, siblings, or even parents. You might think there's no way you can cut them out of your life. If you decide to believe that, you'd make it a true statement and never cut out people that make your life worse. Why people keep toxic people in their lives doesn't make sense to me.

Later in life, I told my dad I would disassociate myself from him if he weren't supportive. I had read a story about a conversation Abraham Lincoln had with his father regarding Abe's goals when he was 15 years old. The story goes that his father told him he'd be nothing more than a frontiersman his entire life and it upset Abe so much, he never spoke with his father again.

I had big goals and couldn't get there with people on my boat rowing in the opposite direction. As you'll read later, it worked! I got to compete at the highest level of Jiu-Jitsu and I got my dream career! But I had to drop some anchors that were holding me back psychologically and emotionally. I had to protect myself from him and many people throughout my life.

Just a year ago, from the time of this writing, I met two people I thought would be great friends, maybe even in my inner circle. However, I cut them off once I got to know them better. Not because I suddenly disliked them but because their negativity and lousy advice would unknowingly hinder me from the direction I wanted my life to go.

When I refer to advice, understand that just being in close proximity to others allows their thoughts and views on the world to impact yours. So, while you may not be actively asking people for advice, understand that during regular conversation and by their habits, you could be poisoned or infected by their viewpoint on life. Don't be bound by the restrictions others have put on themselves, they don't apply to you.

For example, a childhood friend can drink alcohol every night. You both grew up loving the same basketball team, so now you're at a bar - where he likes to watch the games because he's also single - three nights a week watching the games. Before you know it, you're drinking three nights a week, then four, then every day of the week. Your friend never advised you to become an alcoholic in a shitty marriage, but allowing him consistent access to you affected you. At times, people's proximity to you is more harmful than their actual advice.

Remember:

1. It doesn't matter where you came from, it matters that you believe you can get to a better place and have faith that you will because you can.
2. Change the way you see yourself and talk about yourself.
3. Drop anchors. You may love some people, but if they come against your thoughts or actions to better yourself in any way, cut them loose.

Don't let where you came from, what you think of yourself, or small-minded people sow their limiting beliefs into your essence. Fuck that. You have one life and it will go in one of two directions; forward with clear goals and a happy heart or negative with negative people and limited opportunities. I don't know about you, but the latter TERRI-FIES me!

4

HELLO, SPORTS!

DAMN, HE'S FAST!

I WAS AN ODD-LOOKING KID IN 2ND AND 3RD GRADE.
Although still boyish-looking, I already had manly facial features. My
mother hardly got around to getting me haircuts, and my father would
say we'd get to it when we get to it, and we rarely got to it. So I was this
highly energetic platinum-blond afro-sporting-looking kid with cheap
clothes. I stuck out, and not for anything good.

I couldn't change my appearance, both physically or wardrobe-wise, but
I refused to believe that anyone was better than me. Ever since childhood, I did not want to feel looked down upon. A more factual statement is that I wanted to be respected; no, I needed it. The problem was,
I didn't know how to act.

I put it in my head that I was the fastest kid in school. Every recess, I'd
challenge kids to races. Each time, I felt my life was on the line if I didn't
win. I'd run with everything I had, just short of shedding a tear by
holding my breath and nearly closing my eyes till the races were over.
After a while, I stopped losing, even when I raced kids a grade above me.

The school had a P.E. (Physical Education, aka Gym) day every year. In third grade, I had supreme confidence that I would win the big race – being first in going around the most backstops (laps) within ten minutes. I thought, *if there's a world record for this event, I'm breaking it today!*

I took off like the wind as soon as the whistle blew. It didn't take long for me to take the lead. I glanced backward and saw I was creating more distance than the person in second place. I put it in my head that I couldn't call it a win if I didn't lap every other racer. So, in what became the way I did every athletic endeavor, I gritted my teeth and went all out. I guess most kids had found their running rhythm, but not me. I would speed up every time I felt I slowed down. It was much more of a long, arduous sprint than a long-distance race.

I fell when the time went off, more for dramatic effect more than anything else. Many kids asked me, "How many laps did you do?" Again, I answered them between gasps of air – for dramatic effect- and told them the number. As I write this, I don't remember how many laps I did, but I do know that it was one more lap than whoever came in second place. It didn't take long for other kids to tell their parents about the fast, weird-looking new kid in school.

THE PEE WEE LIFE

Around this time, I met the Tecci brothers, Mike, Stephen, and Paul, who would become great life-long friends. Their father was a Pee Wee Baseball coach and asked me to play on his team. At the time, the only experience with baseball I had was being the batboy for Jason's team but I had never played. We discovered in our first practice that I could throw extremely hard and run faster than most kids. I loved being on that team. Sports became a way of life for me, even at that age, most likely because it made me forget about my upbringing and limited the amount of times I got my ass busted.

After that came football season and every Pee Wee dad wanted me on their team. I played running back, and I'll say this as humbly as I can, I was very, very good. I was finally playing a contact sport where I could do some of the hurting without getting in trouble. I was wearing pads and falling on grass, which was nothing compared to the beatings I got from my mom and the punishment I got from my dad. My mentality was to run by them or through them. I didn't play with anger but with an assuredness that I was the toughest kid on the field.

My goals were always aggressive, "I'm getting five touchdowns today, coach!" Some coaches would try to temper my expectations or flat-out tell me I was being selfish, but I would respond with, "No sir, I AM thinking of the team. The other team will have to be amazing to beat us if I score five touchdowns!"

Each coach would constantly remark on my toughness. The truth was, I was deathly afraid of not getting the positive reinforcement and recognition sports were giving me. My teams had our fair share of crybabies, kids that would cry if they messed up a play or got the wind knocked out of them. At times, the kid's dad or worse - mom - would come up to them and either coddle them in front of everyone or scold them to toughen up. I didn't think I had a choice but be tough. My dad would tell me, "You can play, but don't you fucking cry and embarrass both of us!" I feared that disappointing him could mean going back to my mother. Fuck that. I needed the coaches to love me. Sports, or better yet, competing, became my life.

Schools in Texas had their sports teams starting in the seventh grade. The Pee Wee team players would merge to compete to make it on this team. By this time, I wasn't just good; I was "Holy Shit" good. I could bench press as much as the linemen and run faster than the wide receivers. I had seen a girl do a standing backflip before the school year started and practiced it all summer. During football season, I would do standing backflips – at practices and games – with full pads. I had also begun water skiing competitively and thought I'd do that for a living.

My coaches would put me in different track events without me specifically training for them. For some meets, I'd do the 100-yard dash and for others the 2-mile run. Also, no matter what other events I did, I was always on the relay teams. Whatever they wanted me to do, I'd answer, "Yes sir, I'll win at whatever you put me in."

Looking back at it now, it wouldn't surprise me if my coaches had private bets on what I couldn't do. Once I realized my teammates were doing the movements improperly with the discs, I asked to compete. They told me I was too small but they let me try. I out-threw everyone on the team. The next thing I knew, I was handed a pole vault. I did that too.

I broke my collarbone the summer before eighth grade. Before then I had never been to the doctor or dentist. Ever. The doctors told me when I'd be cleared to play football, but his date was past football season. I was devastated.

I asked him if there was anything I could do to speed the healing process. I still can't tell if he was serious, but he told me if I drank a gallon of milk a day, it might help. I began drinking a gallon of milk every day. It was very common for my dad or Jason to be heard yelling in the house, "Fuck, Mike! There's no milk!"

I don't know if it helped, but either way, my bones healed faster than the doctor anticipated. The doctor said I could play but that I would sit out the rest of the year if I had any common sense. Common sense lost to my desire for competition. At first, the coaches said no, but I begged them to at least let me block. They would wrap me up, put some slightly larger pads on me, and threw me on the football field to block and create holes for the running back. I loved it. I didn't have to overthink on the plays. I just had to run in a specific direction and flatten the opposing players in front of me. I wasn't scoring any touchdowns, but I thoroughly enjoyed being back on the field.

HIGH SCHOOL

When I was finished with 8ᵗʰ grade, my father told me the worst news ever. We were moving.

"Noooooooo!"

My life outside of the home was in a groove. I was great friends with the Tecci brothers, each of who earned academic scholarships and are very successful today; all of my coaches loved me, I had lots of friends, and although I wasn't popular with the girls, there were many to choose from. I wanted so badly to win the state championship with my friends, in any sport.

My coaches responded to the news by talking to my dad, trying to convince him to let me live with them during football season. Instead of getting flattered, my dad felt insulted. "Are you saying I'm not doing my job as a father and provider for my family? Even though I'm a simple bricklayer to your eyes because I don't have a fancy job title, my son is and always will be my responsibility. He's coming with his father."

We left the bustling Fort Worth area and moved to sleepy Springtown, Texas. It was only 25 miles west of Ft Worth, but light years behind in terms of society. I felt like I was in an episode of The Twilight Zone when school started; there were no blacks, Hispanics, or Asian students or teachers! I had never experienced anything like that before. As a top-tier young athlete in Texas, I was used to competing with blacks and other races. Most kids in school looked like small-town frat boys while others like farmers, and there I was, this city kid with a Brian Bosworth haircut and an attitude because I didn't want to be there. I soon found out that many people didn't want me there either.

When a new kid (superior athlete) comes into an established community that loves sports, and everyone loves sports in Texas, a good coach must make room for him. That means that other kids get dropped lower on the depth charts. These are kids whose parents the coaches know. Some parents have supported the sports program as boosters or volunteers at parking lots, selling candy bars and fundraisers, team moms coordinating travel and ensuring there are enough Gatorades, and dads running concession stands. The kids who get their positions taken have been playing with their best friends for years. Now, a new, unknown kid from the city whose parents have never supported the program disrupts everything and takes a prestigious spot! No bueno.

Naturally, I didn't know any of that at the time. All I knew was that two-a-days had started and I was practicing with the other freshman while the JV team practiced at another field and the Varsity team practiced at yet another. It took two practices for the freshman coaches to realize they may have something special in me. My football IQ was high, and not only was I beating all the first-year students in the 40 (40 yard dash), I was also beating most of the seniors!

I would excel in football, baseball, and track. As I mentioned earlier, I was a freak athlete who competed with every fiber of his being. I went all out during every practice, game, down, at bat, or track event, of which I would do five events at every track meet.

I got cornered on my third day at school. I had clearly pissed off enough students and parents, so for some reason, a tough kid decided to punish me for it. Like a classic scene of a high school fight, the bully cornered me, and we quickly got surrounded by kids urging us to fight, or in particular, for him to kick my ass. The fight was going to happen whether I wanted it to or not, so I attacked him before he could swing. In short, I kicked his ass, maybe with a little more emphasis than I needed to, so that others wouldn't want to pick a fight with me. As you might expect, I got in trouble for the fight, but it was worth it. No one tried to fight me again. I had established my place in the Hillbilly food chain.

I established a bad reputation as a selfish thug; a kid who only cared about his accolades, had a short temper, and liked to fight. However, my results on the field were undeniable. I only played part of the season for the freshman team before I jumped over JV and played varsity. I had great friends in Ft Worth that I had grown up with. I would go away to visit my friends as often as I could or would call them weekly. We would imagine me coming back and playing with my old team, but that never materialized. I had good moments, some fun times and did make some new friends - primarily seniors and juniors because those are who I played with, but overall, freshman year sucked. Except, I did start to become a little more popular with the girls. I even managed to lose my virginity earlier that year.

My sophomore year was more of the same shit. Being that I played in only varsity teams, most of the friends I had made were seniors who had graduated. Now, I had teammates that were supposed to block for me that hated me. We all knew that sometimes they didn't do their jobs and block when I would run the ball, but the coaches never brought it up. I had a decent season but not nearly as good as I thought I should have. Then, things got much worse.

My dad got into a terrible car accident in April 1992. Although the police officer at the scene said it wasn't his fault, he had a head-on collision with another driver, and a 17-year-old girl died. It fucked him up both physically and psychologically. He was injured so severely that he was bound to a wheelchair, which meant he couldn't work, which meant we were solely dependent on measly checks from the insurance company. We never had much to begin with but that accident caused us to lose nearly every luxury.

With three teenagers, an elementary kid and two adults living off bullshit checks, we couldn't afford to go anywhere, not even for fucking ice cream. True to form, I was the only child that kept bugging my parents for this or that. Although a lot of kids in school hated me, I was popular. I didn't want to wear cheap shit. "This is all we can afford!" became repeated like a broken record. It didn't matter how fast I ran, I thought, my cheap Wal-Mart sneakers would disappear into dust if I go too fast! I preferred to wear old stuff because at least they were name brands.

The weekends were pretty cool, though. My graduated friends would come home some weekends from college and take me out. I had a fake ID and they'd take me to nightclubs in Ft Worth and Dallas. They would say they were sleeping at my house, I'd say I'm sleeping at so-and-so's house, and we'd party all night. I thought hanging out with the older guys was cool, and, as a bonus, with the older guys came the older girls. I wouldn't drink mainly because I never had any drinking money.

I did go to some of their houses and some people were happy I had moved to their town and made their team better. When they found out about my dad's situation, some parents would get me sneakers and gear and even pay the fee for me to play. When my dad asked about the new sneakers, I'd say my friend and I swapped sneakers for a week or some bullshit. He hated rich people and felt nothing was ever for free. If he knew I was a "charity case," he'd never let me keep the gifts.

My sophomore year sucked, but not when compared to my junior year!

5

THE END OF AN ERA

SHE SAID WHAT?

I DIDN'T HAVE A GREAT JUNIOR YEAR IN FOOTBALL. I STILL loved the competition but was exasperated with teammates that didn't care enough to win, or that would not like me so much, they wouldn't play hard when I had the ball. While that part of my life sucked, it was about to get much worse.

I was at a typical high school party. Some kids' parents were away, and kids either paid an adult for booze or used their fake IDs to get it. The music was loud but not loud enough for the cops to be called, and many awkward and uncomfortable conversations were happening between high school boys and girls. I was talking and flirting with a girl a year younger than me, I was 17, and she was 16. We drank, laughed, talked, and sneaked into a bedroom upstairs. We had quiet, uncomfortable, unforgettable and yet, very forgettable sex.

After a day or so, kids approached me, asking if I had sex with that girl. I had no idea how they knew! Well, let me be completely transparent here, mind you, I had been drinking and was young, so maybe I told (bragged to) some of the guys, not realizing that some didn't like me. All I knew was that, as is common in cases like this, the guy (me) is getting high-fived by other guys, but the girl (her) is being called a whore and worse. We weren't even boyfriend and girlfriend, but she was cool and I certainly didn't think that about her.

Her sister was a year older than her and in my grade. I can't explain her motive or thoughts because she never talked to me about the situation. All I know is she threatened to tell on her sister to their parents if she didn't come forward. The girl (her) told me she didn't want to but felt trapped and didn't know what to do.

Weeks later, I'm doing off-season training on the track. Although I didn't enjoy playing football as much, I had my sights on some track records I thought I could break, so as per usual, I was putting the work in. I saw two police officers waiting for me at the finish line. I slowed to a stop when I got near them.

"Are you Michael Alexander?" The taller one asked.

"Yes, sir. Am I in trouble?"

"Well, you're not arrested if that's what you're asking. But we do need to take you to the station to ask you a few questions."

Even though he told me I wasn't under arrest, those assholes put hand-cuffs on me and walked me to their squad car like I was a serial killer. That wouldn't have been a huge deal if the track were somewhere else, but it so happened to be located between the middle and high schools. Also, buses were coming to pick up the middle school kids, so many kids saw the whole thing go down – "Michael Alexander is getting arrested!"

They took me to the police station and asked me to tell them what happened the night of the party. I told them the no-bullshit truth. "Well," the detective said, "she's not exactly saying it was consensual." I couldn't believe my ears – I thought she was cool! They said they'd look into it and held me until my father came to pick me up.

"What the fuck, Mike!" My dad yelled when we got in the car. "How do I get a call saying you raped someone? What is the matter with you?!"

I explained what happened but he cared more about the public perception than what had actually happened. I didn't care much about what he thought about it; honestly, I was just relieved he wasn't kicking me out of the house. It may have been the maddest I had ever seen him.

The girl finally broke down and confessed that what we did was consensual. She told everyone, including her parents, that she participated in the act willingly, and that it wasn't her first... or second... or third time. Sadly, things of that nature often happen to popular high school and college athletes. We'd all like to think the world is better, but it's true; accusations of athletes are common. Common or not, the Baptist Country Coach was upset and had had enough.

Her confession did little to erase the stigma the situation brought on me. I got there as the "bully from the big city," graduated to the, "well, at least he's fast," and digressed to then being the "small-town rapist from the big city." High school fun. Yay.

Her parents and many others would have decided to believe I was a terrible monster instead of the truth. I was so over living in that small-ass town. Our "case" went all the way up to the police chief, who, thankfully, believed our corroborating stories. He even went as far as to talk to the high school faculty and sports coaches, assuring them of my innocence. The football coach hadn't let me practice or play until the matter was resolved. The police chief's words fell on deaf ears regarding our head coach. He had made up his mind as soon as he heard the accusation. He told me not only was I off the team but also suspended from all athletics for a full calendar year. That meant no junior season for track and baseball, and no senior season of football. Fuck, I hated that school!

"But she said I never did anything wrong. So did the police! I didn't do anything wrong!" I argued.

"You think having sex at your age is doing something right? You're suspended, and that's final."

"But why suspend me from all athletics for one year!

"Because I can." The case was closed, as was my high school athletics my junior, and part of my senior year.

THE REST OF HIGH SCHOOL

I planned to go somewhere else for my senior year but Gary Rushing, the best coach I had at the school, convinced me to stay. "You have other goals you've been working for in track and baseball, suffer through this, play those sports and, Mike...dominate. Leave these assholes knowing how special you are. Athletes like you don't come into this town every year."

I did have a terrific senior baseball season, playing catcher and outfielder. I preferred to play catcher but mainly was at center because of my speed, and I could throw the ball at nearly 90 miles per hour. In track, I broke almost every sprinting record held at the school. People could say whatever they wanted about me, but my name was on many record books when I left. I left satisfied that the asshole coach who suspended me for a year would continue to see my name long after I had left.

For years I had posters of my two biggest sports idols hanging on my bedroom wall: Bo Jackson and Deion Sanders, two incredible athletes that played for major league baseball and the national football league. They didn't just play, they dominated. I would always stare at their posters, especially Bo's- wearing football pads and a baseball bat behind his head. However, I came to terms with the fact that being a two-sport professional athlete was not in the cards for me. I often thought things would have been better for me had we stayed in Fort Worth, but none of that mattered. All I wanted to do was get as far away from my house and town as possible after graduation.

Some colleges had sent me letters and tried recruiting me, but I never considered it a legitimate possibility. I didn't know anything about scholarship programs and knew that my dad couldn't afford it. Even if I could go to school for free, I still needed food, clothing, and transportation. Besides, the wrongful allegation would no doubt be discovered, so there was no use in me entertaining college.

I did receive a flyer about joining the Navy when I was still 17. I went to talk to a recruiter and told him I'd love to be a Navy Seal. He told me to return with my dad and complete the paperwork. I didn't do that. My dad was always a little on the negative side and would have told me there was no way I could make it as a Navy Seal. I waited until I turned 18 and filled it out as my own man.

High school graduation came and went with me finishing 80th in a graduating class of 144 students – not the top but not the bottom. The truth was, I was always focused on sports and did the bare minimum on academics. It didn't matter, I reminded myself. I'm not going to college anyway.

A couple of months after, without telling hardly anyone, I left Spring Town, Texas and joined the United States Navy. I was off to Great Lakes, Illinois, on my way to becoming a Navy Seal!

6

MILITARY MAN

THE BOOT

MOST PEOPLE DIDN'T KNOW ANYTHING ABOUT MY HOME LIFE.
They saw me compete or heard about my sports accolades and assumed
I'd get recruited to a university. The truth was, I was a shy and insecure
kid with some serious growing up to do. No one really knew me at all.
My only value was in my potential. And to me, that was very little.

People didn't know my dad would rather us suffer than ask for help. He
hated the thought of people thinking he wasn't doing his job and did
not have a good relationship with the school or other parents that
could have informed us of our options. So, as I discovered over the
years, it shocked many of my friends when they realized I didn't go to
college.

I was excited about the new road ahead, eager to leave Springtown in my
rearview mirror. I started boot camp in July. I was with a bunch of
testosterone-fueled young men out to make a career or serve the country
all of their adult lives as some of their fathers did before them. Everyone
in my Company was a decent human being. As for me, I had two goals –
1 to be a Navy Seal, and 2 – not to attract much attention. Up until

then, being popular brought about unwanted attention and frivolous jealousy.

Goal # 1 blew up before it could get started. Until then, I had never been to a dentist and had only been to a doctor once when I broke my collarbone. The physical examination to join the military is quite extensive. All my tests returned positive; I was *strong like a bull.* However, my eyesight was slightly flawed – I was colorblind! I was told quite matter-of-factly that because of that, I could never try to be a Navy Seal. I was devastated. But what was I supposed to do? I had already signed up, and although my dad and I didn't always see eye to eye, he taught me never to be a quitter. I had to stick it out and hopefully find a job I'd love.

Four companies all shared a courtyard between the barracks. Each company had different tenures; one was two weeks ahead, and another was a month ahead. I was in Company 251 and our sister company was 252. We would compete against them at times. I thoroughly enjoyed the competing events.

A Company Commander told us about the upcoming DC Olympics; an event with various competitions – two of which were relay races, the 1-mile (meaning every racer had to run a lap around the track), and a shorter race, a sprint relay. I had competed in track long enough and was happy to be a spectator for once. In other words, "I didn't wanna do it!"

However, a kid I went to high school with was there and knew I was fast. "Dude, you have to race these guys!"

"No, man, I'm good."

"They're over there talking all this shit. How all white boys are slow!"

"That's a hard pass for me," I reiterated. "Let it go."

"Bro, are you kidding? I thought for sure you were going to do it. I already started talking shit on your behalf. I told them a white boy was going to blow them away!"

I'm not sure how it happened, but someone told the Company Commander, Chief Hurtsberg, and he approached me like a stern father. "Alexander, get your fucking ass out there and test yourself. If you're faster, I want you on the Olympic team. I want to win this thing. End of story."

I raced against the guys from my Company and smoked them all. I made the team. Four experienced track runners comprised our team; we knew how to race, when to start running as the other runner approached, and how to handle the baton. I knew we would win when I realized a guy from our sister company, also on our team, was faster than me. I would always be the last leg in a relay but on this team, he was and I was first. By the time I would hand off the baton, we'd already have a decent-sized lead. By the time the last runner would get it, it was clear we would win. There went my plan of flying under the radar! Shortly after that, I was the Assistant Recruit Chief Petty Officer. I would call the cadence when we marched. I was called the A-ROC.

Boot camp was fun. You go through many events and competitions as a company. If your company wins a particular event, you would get a flag signifying the event. We had collected just about every flag and graduated as an honor company.

FROM MISSISSIPPI TO JAPAN TO HAWAII

I went to Meridian, Mississippi, for Yeoman A School after graduation. If you don't know what a Yeoman is, it's a fancy military word for Administrative Assistant. After all the competition I had done, I was going to wind up a fucking secretary! However, there are seven or eight jobs a recruit could choose from that were SEAL Source Ratings. In other words, picking one of these seven or eight jobs was a requirement if you wanted to be a SEAL. The only job available at the time was.... Yeoman. I didn't care, I was going to be a SEAL no matter what.

I was always a great athlete but I never considered myself much of a leader. Before boot camp, I had gained muscle weight and my posture was different. I was 160 lbs. when I graduated high school and 185 from boot camp. My superiors noticed something in me and made me a Company Commander. I led our company to class every day. Our marches weren't vanilla; we had songs to sing, choreographed marches mixed, and competitions, which we won every time.

I had left a girlfriend back home, and although I had real feelings for her, things were different. I wasn't the bully or kid with a bad attitude from the big city or the rapist; I was a good-looking, muscular, respected man that girls noticed. I wasn't Brad Pitt good-looking, but I was funny, smart, took care of myself, and was quite confident, or at least I appeared to be. I had it easy with the opposite sex to the point that girls had catfights about me. I was messing around with several women, including one of my instructors and a female Marine. I was living La Vida Loca! Then, I read my orders and it really depressed me.

"The USS Beaufort! Fuck man, that's in Sasebo, Japan!"

Luckily for me, one of the girls I was messing with handled the orders. I begged her to do something.

"Come on, I don't want to go to Japan! You have to be able to do something."

"I can't promise anything, but where would you like to go?"

"I have no idea, just not Japan."

She told me a week later somebody changed my orders. "You're going to Pearl Harbor!"

"What? Where?"

"Pearl Harbor! Hawaii, you idiot!"

I was more than thrilled. Although I was born there, my mother moved us when I was a baby. Now I got to return as a man, in the service like my dad was when he was there, and the best part – No Deployments! Hawaii, here I come!

7

HAWAII AND THE BRAWL

ALOHA

I met Jimmy Sullivan in Hawaii, a Chicago kid in the service six months ahead of me, even though he was five years older. He had gotten into legal trouble, and the judge allowed him to join the military or go to jail. He was given this choice because his father was a well-known police officer for the city of Chicago and had a stellar reputation. So, he chose the Navy and ended up meeting me in Hawaii.

We were always together. We would work, work out, and then hit the beach just about every day. He was drawn to me because he was a hell of an athlete and when he saw me breaking the PRT records for the 1.5-mile run, he knew I was one as well. Like a big brother, he significantly influenced me and taught me to be a man. He was a pro boxer and the first person to teach me how to fight. We looked almost identical, so I would use one of his IDs and get into the clubs. It wasn't my first time clubbing; I had been clubbing since I was fifteen, but I wouldn't drink. This time, I'd go and drink and pay a lot more attention to the women. We were great wingmen for each other.

I signed up for the Army Air Assault School, a school which Jimmy had already graduated from, and got to locate and prepare helicopter landing sights, repelled from helicopters, and, among many other cool things, learned a little navigation; I could be dropped anywhere and read a map that would make no sense to anyone else and get home. All in all, I loved being in Hawaii and was fortunate to see where my father had been twenty years earlier.

THE PUNCH

I had been in Hawaii for almost a year and finally had leave for two weeks. During that time, I broke some PRT records, graduated from the Army's Air Assault School, finished training in the ASF (Auxiliary Security Force) Academy, done armed security for a few foreign dignitaries, earned a Top Secret Security Clearance and an Expert Marksman badge with a pistol. I was eager to prove to the people back home that although I had left as a boy, I returned as a man.

I got together with some friends and went to the trendy spot called The Stockyards, home to the best bars and restaurants in the area. There were too many of us to fit in one car so we went in two. I was still trying to get into BUD/S (Basic Underwater Demolition/SEAL Training), so I was in peak physical condition. My friends told some girls about me and they kept me company until the bar closed at 2 AM.

When we left the bar, I noticed a guy an inch away from one of my friend's face that went in the other car. My dumb ass, the fucking hero, ran across the street and got between them.

"What's up?" I said, getting chest-to-chest with him, moving him away from my friend.

"I'm about to kill this stupid motherfucker!" The man pointed to my friend, who he was much bigger than. It didn't take a rocket scientist to realize this guy was a bully. I wondered how many people he had bullied. Well, he wasn't going to do that to me or any of my friends. It was time to show them the man I had become.

"You'll have to get through me." I threatened. My adrenaline was at a fever pitch.

He made a sudden move and my instincts took over. I punched him flush and knocked him out. My friend Jimmy, the pro boxer, would have been proud. In a flash, I won the fight the bully started.

"Mike, get in the car!" someone yelled. I ran back across the street, jumped in the car, and we took off.

On the way home, my friends and I talked about high school fights. If anyone wanted to fight, we'd meet at the peanut field and fight it out. Someone would be declared the winner when it was over and then everyone would go about his or her business. Respect was given and shown the following day. Boys settle their grievances by fighting, that's what we do. None of the fights were life and death. We had no reason to believe this short fight would be any different.

Some friends and I returned to The Stockyards the following weekend and, thankfully, no one mentioned the incident. I returned to Hawaii, assuming all was okay and firmly believing it was over.

I answered an interesting phone call at my desk several months later. The person on the other end acted like he knew me. "Hey Mike, I heard you got in a fight when you were here last time. Are you okay?"

"Ya, I'm okay. Who's this?"

"It's Detective Booker with the FT Worth Police Department. I'm calling to inform you that there's a warrant out for your arrest."

"What's the charge?"

"Aggravated assault with serious bodily injury, it's a felony. I understand you're in Hawaii?" He asked.

"Yes, sir... wait, did you say felony?"

"Well, we aren't going to send anyone all the way to Hawaii to get you, but this charge isn't going away. I advise you to take care of it when you return to Texas, son."

Serious Bodily Injury – what the hell did that mean? I only hit him once but only because he started bullying my friend. We were just boys handling our business. How could I have caused a felony's worth of problems? I would later find out that my one punch had broken his jaw and pushed his bottom teeth through his top teeth, which caused him to require intense surgery.

I hung up and seriously considered never going back to Texas. I informed my legal officer and he recommended I ask for another leave and take care of the matter. I took his advice and was given another leave.

My aunt and uncle agreed to take me to the courthouse the day after I arrived. They owned a bail bonds company and were very familiar with the process. One of my friends picked me up from the airport and we went straight to the bar the day I arrived. The next day, he was driving me to my parent's house so I could meet my aunt and uncle. We got stopped for speeding on the way there. The officer asked us all for our identifications. When he returned to the car, he informed me there was a warrant for my arrest and ordered me to get out of the vehicle and place my hands above my head.

"Yes, sir, I'm aware. We are literally on our way to the courthouse. I'm taking care of it today."

"Like I never heard that before. No, you're taking care of it right now."

I was put in handcuffs, walked to a police car, and the officer held my head down and sat me on the uncomfortable back seat. I felt like a bad guy in a movie. Luckily, my aunt and uncle were able to bail me out. Due to the circumstances surrounding my military assignment, it had been pre-arranged that I would see a judge.

MY DAY IN COURT

I stood in front of the judge and he asked if I had an attorney. I told him I had never been in trouble before so I didn't know I needed one. He instructed me to go to the hallway where there were many attorneys, present my case to them and get legal representation. Almost every lawyer I spoke with said they'd charge me around $3,500.

"Sir," I'd reply, "I'm in the military and don't make that much. There's no way I can afford it."

My salary was exactly $1,300 a month before taxes. All I had of value was a Fossil watch and a red Ford Splash to my name, and I still owed money on that! I had nothing to offer even a half-decent attorney.

I returned to the judge with no representation, feeling like a loser. He told me to go back to the hall and he'd send me someone. True to his word, an attorney, quite annoyed, approached me and took my case.

That's when I realized my punch had done severe damage and pain to the guy I hit, resulting in many medical issues. I left there on felony probation for ten years, but on deferred adjudication, which meant if I completed the ten years without an incident, it would come off my record and I'd never do jail time. I also needed to do 240 hours of community service and pay a $1,500 fine during the length of the probation. I'm sure, to the victim, it wasn't nearly enough to make up for what I had done to him, but I was willing to do whatever was required to complete my sentence without any incidents. I returned to Hawaii with my tail between my legs but ready and willing to put everything behind me.

Unfortunately, there was a huge disconnect between some people who worked in that courthouse and me. I told them I was in the military and being that there is a military base in Fort Worth, they assumed I was stationed there. I assumed they knew I flew in from Hawaii, where I was when the detective first called me, but they didn't. Great communication Texas Justice Department! A few months later, I received a call from another officer telling me there was another warrant for my arrest!

"For what now? I didn't do anything!" I exclaimed.

"Exactly. You didn't do anything, including not appearing in front of your probation officer."

"But I'm in Hawaii!"

"This matter is not going away. Come back to Texas and get it resolved."

The legal officer for the Navy went back and forth with the State of Texas on my rights, duties, and freedom for six months. Finally, the Navy backed down. They gave me a General Discharge that would upgrade to Honorable in 6 months. I was devastated.

I sat dazed and confused as I prepared to pack my gear and return to Texas. Everything I had planned and worked for had slipped through my fingers in the blink of an eye. Things I thought were absolutes, like attending BUD/S, were not even an option.

On the sad flight home, I remembered the many times my mother used to beat me. Once, she smashed my head into the oven door to prove she was stronger and the dominant figure at home. Not only had she tried to kill me, twice, she also treated me like a human rag doll, yet, she wasn't a felon. Those weren't fair fights. I had hit a guy who was ready to hit someone else. He had made the first move. That was a fair fight.

Or, was everyone right about me? Did I have the same violent demons my mother struggled with? Then I had another thought: at what point does potential disappear? When is it too late to judge someone?

I headed back home with no military experience on my resume and no schooling beyond a high school diploma. I stuck up for a friend, fought a fair fight, won the fight, but somehow had lost big time.

8

BANG!

LUBBOCK

I RETURNED HOME FEELING HURT AND SAD ABOUT HOW MY military career ended. I enjoyed the Navy, even if I never became a Seal. I'd never been one to sulk or cry about things for too long, so I looked at my prospects thinking, *what's next?* I wanted to be a policeman and be on a SWAT unit. That idea got shot down immediately. I literally didn't know what the hell I was going to do with my life.

I have a cousin named Kevin, who's a few years older than me. He's a big guy, 6'4, 240 pounds, and very charismatic. He reached out to my dad to see what I was up to and when my dad told him I wasn't doing much, he connected with me.

"Mike, I'm killing it at my job. I sell modular homes for a great company. I think I made like $22,000 last month." He said enthusiastically.

"Good for you, man."

"Ya, but this call isn't about me, it's about you. You have all the potential in the world. Come with me to Lubbock and I'll show you the ropes."

"Lubbock?"

"Cuz, I got promoted in a year. I'll put you on the fast track to get promoted too. I'll make $160,000 this year. I can teach you how to do this; you'd be great at it. What do you say?"

I didn't have recruiters banging on my door or any decent options. "Fuck it. I can be there in a week." I drove the four and a half hours from Fort Worth to Lubbock as soon as my truck shipped from Hawaii.

He didn't lie to me about the money he was making or the type of money I could, but he didn't tell me the work schedule. We worked seven days a week, from 9 AM to 7 PM. I started with a $350 weekly draw and increased to 100% commission. It took a little while for me to get going but Kevin wasn't charging me rent and I had no other options, so I went all in. We went hard every single day.

Money started to come in for me after a couple of months. I made $7,000 one month and then $10,000 the following month. No one had ever taught me financial literacy, so I started spending it when I started making more money than ever. The higher-ups in the company noticed me and told me I had tremendous potential to make it big with them. I had heard that I had so much potential but it was usually in athletics. Now, I was making money and proving to Kevin's boss that he was right about me.

We would work hard every day and party hard every night. I'd feel great coming back home and buying my friends drinks like a boss, all the while driving a Corvette the following week, barely able to afford the gas because I would spend all my money. I didn't save or invest – I worked, partied, bought drinks, and slept with women. Two years later, true to Kevin's word, I was promoted to Sales Manager at Fort Worth, back home!

THE SWEDE

I went out every night when I was 21 until I was 23. I never had a steady girlfriend. I'd always keep a bag packed in my car because I never knew where I'd wake up. I didn't know if the girls liked me because of my car, my sports reputation, or because I bought them drinks, and I didn't care. Fort Worth was a college town and many pretty but broke college girls gave me a lot of attention, which was good enough for me.

One night, I met a beautiful woman who I referred to as, The Swede. She was a gorgeous, brilliant, bubbly blonde with great energy, a great job, no kids, and level-headed – I was shocked that she liked me. We spent the next thirty days with each other since the day when we met. She was 33 and I was 23, and every day I pinched myself; I couldn't figure out how a woman like her could like me the way she did. I was hooked.

I decided to have her meet Kevin and his wife, so we made plans to go to The Stockyards for dinner and drinks. When she and I would hang out, she would have little to no alcohol. That night, maybe because she was nervous about meeting some of my family members, she drank. Kevin and I were veterans in the drinking game, so it was amusing when she got a little loud in the restaurant. I thought it was cute and I'd tease her about it afterward.

We left the restaurant and went to a popular bar and that's when she started to exhibit behaviors I had never seen from her. She kept buying shots and got more than tipsy. A guy bumped into her and said, "Excuse me," but instead of understanding that we were at a crowded bar and people would inadvertently bump into each other, she pushed him and yelled, "Don't fuck with me. My boyfriend will kick your fucking ass!"

I had never seen her act like that and didn't like what I saw. I went to the bathroom and figured I'd run to the bar across the street, where I would hang out with friends. Sure as shit, a couple of my friends were there and they bought me a drink. I hung out with them for about an hour. When I returned, Kevin gave me a look to let me know he wasn't kidding, "We're gonna call it a night."

We had driven in Kevin's truck, so he drove us back, with The Swede and I in the back seat. Suddenly, Kevin's wife half turned to The Swede and started yelling at her. In her defense, The Swede did embarrass us with her behavior. Then Kevin's wife started yelling at me for leaving her with them for an hour, during which time, The Swede argued with several people. Then The Swede started yelling at her for yelling at me. I don't recall who threw the first punch or slap but they scuffled a little in the truck until Kevin and I, holding back our laughter, pulled them apart.

I didn't think anything earth shattering happened, I figured we wouldn't let them two drink together again. I wasn't too happy with The Swede and told her I would stay at Kevin's house that night. She stumbled to get into her car.

"If you don't drive her home," Kevin said, "she aint getting home."

On the way to her house, she started to cry – hard; stating that she was 33 and never had kids and that she had never even had a relationship for more than six months and now I was going to break up with her. "I just want to fucking die." She repeated several times. I just wanted to get home without getting stopped by the cops, I was still on probation. I tried to calm her down but she was inconsolable, so I let her ramble on.

We got to her house and she changed into a t-shirt and asked if I was staying. I didn't want to take another chance driving, so I said yes, stripped down to my underwear, and went to the sofa. I heard her sobbing from outside the bedroom so I went to the bed and hugged her from behind. "Shh, just sleep it off. Everything is going to be okay."

I heard the nightstand drawer open and close but didn't think much of it. I kissed the back of her head and then everything went haywire!

GUN SHOT

BANG!

A mega-loud bang filled the room and a piercing flash of light left me momentarily blinded. The boom was so loud I could barely hear anything except the ringing in my ears. I pulled away from her and waited for my eyes to adjust. I noticed that the nearest window was slightly opened and thought someone must have gotten close and tried to shoot us through the window.

"Hey, someone's shooting at us!" I yelled as I jumped out of the bed. I could barely hear myself talk, almost like when your face is not in the water but your head is, so you speak but sound muffled because your ears are underwater. It was an odd, horrible sensation. I still saw spots as I searched the wall for the light switch while calling her name. I turned the light on and realized that she hadn't moved.

With my eyes blinking and gaining full sight, I walked slowly toward her and noticed blood pouring down her face. I looked out the window and wondered who could have done something like that.

"HOLY SHIT! I'll get you some help!"

I scrambled over to find the cordless she kept in the bedroom but didn't find it quickly so I ran to the kitchen and picked up the phone I knew was there and dialed 9-1-1 with jittery fingers.

When the operator picked up the call, I yelled, "Someone just shot my girlfriend!"

"Is the person still there?" the female voice said. I had trouble hearing her so she had to repeat herself several times.

"No, whoever did it shot from outside the open window."

After a moment, the voice said, "I dispatched the police and ambulance. Do you know if your girlfriend is still breathing?"

"Let me check!"

"Sir! Sir! Don't leave the phone!"

It was too late. I put the phone down and ran to see if The Swede was dead or alive.

"Hey, can you hear me?"

I approached her and had to wade through the many throw pillows she would keep on her bed and throw them on the floor when it was time to sleep. She didn't respond. I clapped in front of her face as loud as I could and she blinked and then gasped for air. I started asking her questions but she was in a severe daze. She leaned down and rummaged for something under the pillows. When she moved a pillow aside, I realized what had happened. She had shot herself! Below me, on the floor, was a Daringer 25. She extended her fingers and reached for it again.

I quickly grabbed the gun and tossed it to the far side of the room. She was losing a lot of blood and would be unable to pick up the gun so I ran back to the kitchen and grabbed the phone.

"Ma'am, I think she shot herself."

"Sir, did you see the gun?"

"Yes."

"Listen to me, this is very important – don't touch the gun!"

"I had to! She was reaching for it so I threw it across the room." Panic seeped in quickly but everything was happening so fast and I was still recovering from being about an inch away from a fired revolver.

"Don't go back in the room. The police should be knocking on your door in sixty seconds."

Still in my underwear, I opened the door and waited for help. Police officers arrived first, followed by EMTs. A uniformed cop put both hands on my shoulders and gently walked me out of the way – I was in such a daze I didn't move out of their way to get into the house. The same officer then picked up the phone, told the operator they were there, and hung up. The EMTs rushed by me and went to the room and then a detective; looking like a classic detective with worn shoes, slacks, buttoned shirt, and loose tie, who I didn't recall walked in, walked out of the room and stopped in front of me.

"Tell me how the gun got to the other side of the room." He demanded.

"I went to see if she was okay. The gun was on the floor next to her and when she came to, she reached for it. I didn't know if she would shoot herself again or me. I beat her to the gun and threw it to the other side of the room. Then I ran to the phone to tell the woman she was alive." I said through frantic sobs and tears.

The detective looked at me all of three seconds before he made his accusation. "You shot that girl. Admit it!"

I looked at him in shock. There I was, crying and totally dejected, and this asshole was going to try to pin this on me? Oh, hell no. "Fuck you!" I yelled. "All I did was call you guys to help her."

"I don't believe it." He said.

"Fuck you!" I pointed at him and took a step toward him. In an instant, the cops grabbed me and threw me to the ground. I didn't resist and they hogtied me, tying my feet and hands together behind me while I lay on my stomach. For a moment, I knew the matter would be cleared shortly but then I remembered, *Fuck, I touched the gun!*

They ran my name through their system. The detective told the uniform cops, "He's on felony probation." It was as if that was enough to indict me. I couldn't believe what was happening. How does my life change so quickly?

A paramedic came out, blood on his gloves, "We need you in here, detective." In what was probably ten minutes, although it felt like an hour, the detective came back out and motioned to a uniformed officer.

"We're going to un-cuff you," he said to me. "But don't fucking move. Don't touch anything. Sit with your hands on your legs." After I got un-hogtied, I sat down as he instructed. "We tied you because you made an aggressive move toward me. But I'm going to forget that and try to figure this out. Now, very calmly, with as much detail as you remember, tell me what happened."

"I told you already." It flashed through my head to lawyer up. He had already accused me of shooting her. What if I slipped and said something wrong? My nerves and emotions were all over the place.

"There is a hole in your girlfriend's head. You two were the only ones in the room and YOU touched the gun, meaning your fingerprints are on it. Now, what happened?"

I tried to calm myself down and tell him every detail I could recall. The truth was, it had happened so fast. After I finished, he waited for a while, as if allowing me to come clean or change my story. When he realized I was done speaking, he sighed loudly and told me, "She's not dead. She's actually talking, and although she's not very coherent, she's saying she did this to herself. I'll still need to take you with us."

"Can I make a phone call?"

They rushed her in an ambulance and I got my second ride in a police car, this time on the front seat, where the officer nonchalantly asked questions about our relationship. When we arrived, he instructed me not to touch the door, ran around the car, and opened it for me.

They sat me in the hospital wearing a paper gown with instructions not to move or wipe my hands. They eventually tested my hands to determine if I had fired the weapon. It came out negative. Then they tested my face since I told them I was close to the muzzle. It came out positive and corroborated my story.

The detective came to my room. "Although she tried, your girlfriend didn't commit suicide. She had placed the gun behind her ear, where the thickest part of the skull is. And, because she didn't have a very powerful gun, the bullet didn't penetrate the skull. The good news for you is, she still maintains your innocence in this ordeal."

Kevin, whom I called, got there at about the same time a psychiatrist came to check on me to make sure I was okay psychologically. He told me he had treated The Swede before and that she suffered from bipolar manic-depressive. "You're lucky she was on alcohol and not drugs. She felt she had disappointed you, so, being drunk, she shot herself. If she were on drugs and thought you were disappointed in her, in her manic state, she would have shot you."

He asked if I would see her after this. I answered, "I don't think so."

"Listen very carefully to what I'm going to say. I can hold her here for 72 hours, the longest I can hold anyone for evaluations, but then I have to let her go. This should give you enough time to go to her house and remove everything that's yours, including pictures, gifts, trinkets – everything. Then, Michael, and this is important, don't ever talk to her again. Ever. I can almost assure you that this will happen again but with a worse result if you stay with her."

I went with Kevin and took everything that would make her remember me. He then dropped me off at my apartment, where my roommates were awake, waiting to hear the whole story, even though it was around 5 AM.

"Thanks, Kev, I appreciate you, cuz," I said earnestly.

"My wife did say she was a crazy bitch."

I gave him a stern look.

"What? Too soon?"

9

TIME TO GROW UP

MY FIRST COMPANY AND FIRST MARRIAGE

THE INCIDENT WITH THE SWEDE SHOOK ME TO MY CORE. FOR the first time, I had a serious evaluation of my life. I couldn't stop but think - *most of what happened to me was someone else's fault.*

My mother was an addict that tried to murder me, which would probably scar anyone else for life. My father worked hard but didn't understand me and I did not want to end up like him. He was devastated at what I went through but also made light of the situation, deflecting any trauma that could have come from that incident. Most of my football coaches were incompetent, if not complete idiots, with a few being straight-up assholes. My roommates and good friends were joking about the incident that nearly got me killed or in prison for murder. I had been playing behind the eight ball since I was born.

The same thought continued to pop up in my mind – *most of what happened to me was someone else's fault.*

I realized it was time to take control of my life and stop allowing myself to blame whatever bad came to me on other people. I didn't know what to do; I just knew I had to do something different. I had to grow the hell up.

My father told me, "You want to grow up? Settle down, get married, and start having kids."

He may as well have told me to jump off a bridge. My life was chaotic; I had no money in the bank, no house, and now a crazy ex-girlfriend that nearly killed herself. I wasn't exactly marriage material. All the times people had told me I had potential had not materialized. But it's strange how life brings you opportunities when you start thinking differently.

A few months later, I met Sheila. She was four years older, divorced, and had a four-year-old daughter. I met her at a bar and made her laugh a few times. We exchanged numbers but didn't call one another. A couple of weeks later, she walked by me at another bar and I recognized her, but not entirely. It was one of those, "Where do I know you from?"

After about a minute of wondering how I knew her – we had been drinking quite heavily the night we met – it kicked in. "Wait. You're 28, work in the staffing industry, um, hold up, you have a four-year-old daughter, and your name is..."

"Sheila," She said with a smile.

We got a bite to eat after the bar closed and began dating. It didn't take her long to tell me I was too smart to do what I was doing. I brushed it off at first; after all, I was making much better money than ever before and certainly more than most of my friends. I was good. But she challenged me to do more with my life in her own way.

If you've read my story to this point, you already know I'm not one to run from a challenge.

I asked a few people what they thought of me getting into the construction cleanup business. My dad, who told me to settle down, told me I wasn't ready to own a company. He looked at me as if I were out of my mind. Almost everyone else gave me the same bullshit advice – "Start small, don't take on too much, don't take risks."

I thought, *start small? That only gets you small wins. There's no money in small wins. Fuck that!*

I financed a bobcat, trailer, and truck and swung for the fences. I'd talk with people about things I'd never done and promised them my company would handle it. As money came in, I invested and got a dump truck, then another, and then another.

Someone asked if I could tear down a building. Hell, I'd never torn one down before. "You bet your ass we can! How fast do you need that son of a bitch to come down?" The problem was I didn't know how to price it. The guy took a chance on me, offered me $25K to do it, and didn't take any other bids on the job. We tore down that 2-story cinder block building and hauled everything off in four days. This was 2001, when $25K was much more money than today. I knew I could build a solid and lucrative company if I could get some investment money.

Sheila saw the money come in and was proud I had rolled the dice on myself. However, even though she had perfect credit, she was not about to invest in anything unless it was with her husband, not her boyfriend. I made the business decision then and there to marry her. I know, it's probably the least romantic proposal story in history, but that's how it went down.

Shortly after that, we got married at a Justice of the Peace. No one was happier than Megan, her daughter. She and I got extremely close. Sheila had, as she put it, "a real job," and I was self-employed, which meant I could change my schedule, so I would take and pick up Megan from school every day. I would take her for ice cream, parks, and toy shopping. I wanted to be the parent I felt I didn't have. She thought her stepdad was a superhero and I thought my stepdaughter was the sweetest little girl ever.

True to her word, Sheila invested more money; true to my word, more significant projects started coming in, meaning more money came in. Unfortunately, I was still the same guy. I was still spending money as fast as it came in and would go out drinking with my buddies most nights. I'd never make it home some nights. At around five months into the marriage, we had "The Talk." We were divorced a month later.

Still, we had a cash cow in our hands, so we tried to run the business together, but as hard as we tried, we couldn't get the emotions out of the business decisions. After another talk, we agreed to sell everything. Eighteen months after I started the company, I shut it down, selling our contracts, equipment, and everything else that came with it. We paid off everyone we owed and went our separate ways.

SEMI-PRO BALL

I had managed to stack some money, so I bought a Porsche and decided to see what I'd do next. It had been years since I had delved into anything athletic, and a friend told me that the Fort Worth Texans, a semi-pro football team, were having tryouts. I worked hard, got back in shape, and tried out as a slot receiver. To my surprise, I made the team!

I was now a professional athlete except without the millions of dollar contract and my face on a cereal box. The pay was crap but our team had good sponsors. I enjoyed being part of a team again. We'd practice hard four nights a week, travel, and go out afterward. There was no shortage of groupies. I loved it. I figured there'd be plenty of time to grow up later. I got a job that could work around my schedule and went all in.

I didn't start initially but got on the field in the special team's group. A few weeks later, the person above me in the depth chart got hurt and I got the nod. He never got his spot back. I was fast, had good hands, and had a higher football I.Q. than most on the field. I knew everyone's assignments on every play. We had a great quarterback who had a stellar college career and great receivers – one ended up playing for the Green Bay Packers. Another teammate was a guy named Brad Imes. He was a big, 6'9, 290-pound wild man that had played left tackle at Mizzou. We became great friends.

It took a while, but I earned the quarterback's trust, especially at the end of games. The other teams would "smartly" double-cover our receivers, leaving the white boy one-on-one. The problem for them was I was always too quick and shifty for a linebacker to keep up with. When the game was most often on the line, I'd win my matchup and score us a touchdown or get us the first down to kill the clock and win the game. There was a famous Dallas Cowboys star named Terrell Owens, who went by his initials. T.O. Because of my late-game heroics, they started calling me O.T. because I always delivered at the end of the game or Over-Time.

IN THE CLUB!

As much as I enjoyed playing football and hanging out with my team-mates, I knew the NFL was not in the cards for me. I had another self-reflecting moment and accepted that I had to try that grown-up thing again. With no other real-world experience outside of construction, I joined a flooring company as a field supervisor while I was still playing.

Then, as life has it sometimes, I found myself at the right place at the right time. A client needed floors faster than we had ever done them. I liked the guy and wanted to help him, so, being the field supervisor, I told him we could do it. My boss was pissed, "It's you that gave your word. So now you will stay there day and night; you won't ruin the company's reputation!"

My team and I started on a Thursday, worked around the clock, and finished it by Saturday. The builder that needed the help was a construction company based out of Chicago. Their origin story, which is 100% true, is that an old gangster family tried to go legit and got into construction. After meeting them, I didn't doubt it for a second. Based on performing the 'miracle of the floors,' they offered me a job as a Superintendent. I was officially in the club.

I interviewed with a man named James Arledge and got hired. Thank-fully, he has the heart of a true mentor, he's not one to throw anyone to the wolves or do what other people do, throw them to the deep end to see if they could swim. Instead, he had me shadow him for 90 days and taught me the right way to build houses. He was single and older than me, but he occasionally hung out with the team and me. Friends aside, he didn't let me come to work late, regardless of how late we stayed out. Unfortunately, I didn't have the Michael Irvin gene, which could let you party all night, come to work early the next day, and produce magic.

"Listen, Mike, take this more serious. You have something special, a great POTENTIAL to be a great builder."

I appreciated him saying that to me but there was that word again – potential. I had heard I had it over and over again but I was still more interested in partying than anything else. When the hell is this potential going to materialize?

After 3 ½ seasons, I left the football team and took life much more seriously. It was time for me actually to start growing up. I just didn't know how.

10

VIOLATED

HELLO, I'M THE DEVIL

A VOICE INSIDE ME TOLD ME IT WAS TIME TO LIVE UP TO MY potential, but I didn't know how to do that, so I just did what I knew – work, work out, and party. My focus narrowed to building houses, working out, and going out. I was a good student, so my house-building career was going great, especially with all the experience I had accrued running my own business. I started to work out heavily and got up to 225 lbs. of muscle, yet I still went out almost every night of the week.

About six months after the divorce, I met a beautiful woman at a bar who lived the same lifestyle as me – working and drinking. Her name was Kerry; little did I know she was the devil incarnate. We didn't hit it off immediately, but we would joke and flirt when we'd bump into each other at different bars. After about six months, we went on our first official date. I fell for her... hard.

SEASON 2

Season 2 of The Ultimate Fighter started on Spike TV during this time. I mention it because my close friend, Brad Imes, made the show. He only had three professional fights prior to the show, so we were all excited for him to make it on a national stage. Two champion fighters were chosen as coaches, Matt Hughes and Rich Franklin. Due to Brad's inexperience, he was picked last and was expected to lose his first fight. To their surprise and my delight, Brad ran through the competition and made it to the Finals. I went with a buddy of mine to Las Vegas to see the finale. That's when I got my first taste of the UFC.

I was at AJ Steakhouse when Dana White came in with the cast to buy them all dinner. I introduced myself as Brad's friend, and we chatted for about 30 minutes. If Dana White gives you that much time, people will assume you are somebody. One particular guy said he recognized me and asked for my autograph. I smiled and wondered if I should play along but then told him he must have me confused with someone else. That should have been the end of it, right? Not for this guy!

He was a little upset that I wouldn't sign his autograph. Dana looked over as the guy got a little louder; I shrugged to Dana as if to say, *I don't know who the hell he thinks I am.* Dana smirked, and I smiled widely. I think the guy took my smile to mean that I was blowing him off because he got louder and yelled at me in a high-end restaurant for not giving him my autograph! He got so loud the manager came to see what the commotion was about.

I was about to explain to the manager that I wasn't famous, but he stopped me in mid-sentence and said to the guy that was yelling, "He doesn't have to give you an autograph if he doesn't want to!" The guy got upset at the manager and threatened him. The manager told him to leave, and the guy touched the manager's head. I had no idea that the restaurant would have bouncer-like employees, but as soon as that guy touched the manager, two big guys quickly snatched the guy up and practically threw him out of the restaurant. The manager then apologized to me and offered to comp my meal.

Brad and I ended up at the Spike TV after party and then at Joe Stevenson's after-party at Tao. Most of the fighters there were surprised that I wasn't a fighter or a coach. I had heard it enough times that I told Brad, "Maybe I should give this MMA thing a shot."

Brad agreed, "Finally. Let's get you started. I'll find you a good gym."

Brad and Rashad Evans' fight was epic! A six-figure contract with the UFC was on the line, and both men gave it all they had. In the end, Rashad won by split decision. However, Brad performed so well that Dana gave him a UFC contract as well. All of a sudden, MMA had come very close to home.

THE SLAP

Not long after the Vegas trip, I went to watch the high school state championship games with some of my friends who were high school coaches. Kerry called me excitedly to tell me about the new car she bought and wanted to know when I would get home. I told her the guys I was with wanted to watch every game, so I would get back at around two in the morning.

We ended up leaving earlier, so I went to the bar Kerry was at. She looked surprised to see me, told me to hold on a minute, and disappeared. Around 20 minutes passed, and a friend asked if I was waiting for Kerry. I told her I was, and she told me a guy had her by the arm and wouldn't let her go. An officer was near us and overheard the conversation. We both went in search for her.

I outdistanced the cop and saw a stranger holding Kerry's arm, just as the girl said. I can't put into words the feeling that came over me; it wasn't jealousy; it was a need to protect my girl. I wanted to punch the guy's lights out, but I open-hand slapped him hard instead.

"What do you think you're doing?" the cop yelled from behind me.

"This asshole is holding on to my girlfriend against her will!" I replied.

The cop took two seconds to assess the situation and realized I was telling the truth. "Go home." Luckily, the guy didn't press charges. I was, after all, still on probation.

Kerry and I went home, and she went on and on about not knowing why the guy would do that to her. As I stated earlier, Kerry was a beautiful woman, so I chalked it up that some dumbass drunk guy fell in drunk-love with her and probably didn't even realize he was holding her against her will. That shit happens when you're girlfriend is drop-dead gorgeous but is also a chronic flirt.

The guy called me a few weeks later, saying he wanted to clear the air. "I don't know what happened, man. I've been trying to talk to you for a week because Kerry hasn't responded to me. The reason I was grabbing her is because I've been seeing her for almost three months. She told me she couldn't go out often, and I was fine with that, so we only see each other when she can. I didn't understand what was happening when she told me she was leaving with another guy. Then, you came over and hit me!"

I was stunned.

"Are you dating her?" he asked.

"We've been dating for two years!"

He was trying to be cool; it's not as if he knew she was in a relationship. Either way, I didn't want to know anything more about him or Kerry and told him not to call me again.

Kerry confessed and cried, but there was no way I would ever stay in a relationship where a girl cheated on me once, let alone have an affair for three months. Fuck no. She kept trying to get in touch with me, but as far as I was concerned, we were over, and it was final.

A week later, the guy called again, but this time, he wasn't being cool at all. He smugly told me that he and Kerry are back together and that he did some research on me, which is bullshit. The only research he did was to hear what Kerry had to say about me. "I hear you have your own business and are doing well. I also heard you're on probation."

"And?" I asked.

"Meet me tomorrow with four thousand dollars in cash, and I won't press charges."

I nearly squeezed my phone in half, "How about I meet you tomorrow and slap you four thousand more times?"

IT'S ONLY A CLASS C MISDEMEANOR

A uniformed police officer came to my house a few weeks later and informed me that the guy had pressed charges.

"Are you here to arrest me?"

"No." He replied, "It's only a Class C Misdemeanor. But you need to take care of it, or I or another cop will have to come back and take you down."

The cop was quite nonchalant about it, so I blew it off. A different police officer came to my house the following week and told me I was under arrest.

"I talked to a cop who told me it was only a Class C Misdemeanor. I was going to take care of it." I replied.

"Honestly, I'm not aware of any of that. I'm here because of the warrant out on you for violating your probation."

I hired an attorney and bonded out of jail. My lawyer let me know that the state of Texas took probation violations very seriously. "I know," I said, "that's why I hired you."

I stupidly called Kerry and blasted her for telling that jackass my personal information and that now her stupid boyfriend pressed charges on me.

"Well, you should have paid him!"

It was then that I realized two things.

One – Kerry was behind this whole thing.

Two – I should have paid the fucking guy.

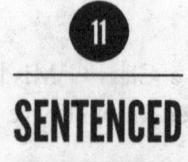

11

SENTENCED

SEMI-VOLATILE

I HAD BEEN ON PROBATION FOR MORE THAN NINE YEARS OUT of a ten-year sentence. I was squeaky clean in the eyes of the law for almost a decade. Then, in the blink of an eye, the law had me in its crosshairs. I was in disbelief. I was doing well, helping people and society by building homes. I wasn't a thug or a gangster. I didn't do or sell drugs; I wasn't a thief or a con man. This should not have been happening to me.

News of my legal trouble got out to my friends and acquaintances. Everyone was shocked, including Kerry's so-called friends. As I waited on a court date, some of Kerry's friends told me about what Kerry had done behind my back during the two years we dated.

I knew we were in a semi-volatile relationship the entire time I dated her. For example, we would make plans to meet at a restaurant; I'd go at the designated time, wait there, wait some more, then realize she wasn't going to show up, go to a club not to waste any more time, not see her all night, fight with her or not talk to her for a few days, see her out, have amazing make-up sex and we'd be good.

My friends hated her. Not so much for her, but because I would let her stand me up, not show up, rant to them about her, only for them to see me lovey-dovey with her again the next day. The Mike they knew before would have never put up with a girl telling him to mind his business about her Vegas trip.

According to her friends, Kerry's problem wasn't that she wasn't punctual; she was a fucking cheater. She would tell me she was going to go on a girls-only weekend trip only so that she could hook up with a guy. They also said to me that while they didn't know where she would be when she didn't show up to our dinner dates, they would have bet their left legs she was with another guy. Someone told me that she had told her that she asked a lawyer what she had to say to get me to jail!

COURT, AGAIN

The court date was set and my lawyer and I were as prepared as we would ever be. The truth is, I slapped the guy. However, we felt when we told the judge he tried to extort me, the judge would throw it out. The problem was we needed evidence we didn't have. Suffice it to say, I walked into the courtroom with a nice suit but almost shaking from fear.

The prosecuting attorney did his best to paint me as a violent man based on why I was on probation in the first place. Then he told the court I was in a jealous rage and that the other guy was lucky a police officer was there, "Look at him. I shutter to think what Mr. Alexander would have done to Mr. Smith if the police officer hadn't been there to save him."

We testified and proved that Kerry and I had been dating for two years and she had been cheating on me for three months with Mr. Smith. We told the court the situation that night of a guy I had never seen physically restraining my girlfriend. We also implored the court to consider my record for the last nine plus years, "Do the last ten years look like an unhinged man who flies off the handle and attacks people?"

My lawyer's last comments were about the phone call the guy made in an attempt to extort me for four thousand dollars. That seemed to perk the judge up. She recalled Mr. Smith to the witness stand and was asked, under oath, if he demanded I pay him that money. All Mr. Smith had to do was answer that he never said that and I would have been screwed. However, he came clean and admitted he tried to extort me.

The judge asked, "Why did you feel he owed you money?"

Mr. Smith replied, "Well, he embarrassed me in front of everyone and I missed two days of work because of him."

The judge said, "You were physically restraining a woman, so I won't pay you for being embarrassed. What do you do for work that made you miss out on four thousand dollars?"

She told him he had no right to demand or expect money from me except perhaps two days' worth of work. "We are here because he didn't pay the money you tried to extort from him!"

My lawyer and I gave each other a look and I forced myself not to smile. We had executed our plan! Mr. Smith agreed in court that he, and by proxy, Kerry, attempted to extort me. I knew for sure the judge would throw the case out!

I got called back to the stand, and the judge waited a while before she spoke as if she wasn't sure what to say. "Mr. Alexander, I'm very sorry Mr. Smith attempted to extort you. However, that's not why we're here. You are here because you are on probation and when you physically assaulted Mr. Smith, you clearly violated said probation."

Fuck. I thought she called me up there to tell me she would throw the case out!

"This is what I'm going to do," she continued. "I'm going to put this matter in pre-sentence investigation. A court appointed official is going to interview many people who know you and details of this case. This official will give me a full report and I'll make my decision on this case based on those findings. You are free to go, Mr. Alexander, but stay in touch with your attorney; he'll inform you of our next court date."

I left there having gone through a myriad of mixed emotions. I felt I was doomed when the prosecuting attorney tried to label me as a dangerous, jealous man with a violent streak. Then, I felt elated when Mr. Smith admitted he had tried to extort me. Then, I didn't know how to feel, being that an investigator would talk to people who knew me. That, by itself, was a little embarrassing. All in all, I considered it a minor win that I was free to go but I wasn't doing cartwheels.

My name came up in a random drug test about two weeks later. It had happened periodically in the last nine plus years, so I wasn't thinking this was anything out of the ordinary. They ended up arresting me again, this time without bond, meaning I would not be let out until I saw the judge again.

The guy who had done the pre-investigation in the case visited me in jail the following day. I ravenously but meticulously read everything on the 24 pages. The first 23 pages were great. However, Mr. Smith and Kerry made a statement that they were afraid that I was going to retaliate on the last page. The investigator told me not to worry too much, especially since everything else looked good for me. "Based on my experience, the worst case scenario? The judge makes you wait in jail 30 days to show Mr. Smith that she takes his well being seriously and that you'll use that time to cool down."

THE SENTENCE

December 20, 2006. I stood in front of the judge, alongside my attorney, already thinking of where I would go that weekend and how I would never get in trouble again.

"Did you read the results of the investigation?"

"I did, your honor."

"They're scared you are going to retaliate. Are they right?"

"No, your honor. I had a wonderful life before them and look forward to returning to it. They have no reason to fear seeing me ever again."

"I believe you. My heart tells me that you wouldn't retaliate."

I let out a sigh of relief slowly so that no one could see it.

The judge then looked at the people in the room, "I have a burden to protect our society and everyone in it. When a case like this comes before me, and I'm unsure exactly what to do with it, I go to my family. I tell them facts of the case, without mentioning names, of course. I take their advice seriously because they understand these are real people with families I talk to them about.

One of them asked me what would happen to me if I let a man with a history of violence go free after clearly violating probation and he hurt the two people who told the court they are afraid of. I told them I could get disbarred. The other family member told me I had my answer."

She looked back at me. "I do believe you wouldn't hurt them, Mr. Alexander. But my heart doesn't make the decisions, the letter of the law does and I'm tasked to interpret it for the safety of everyone. Therefore, I hereby sentence you to four years in prison."

Twenty-three pages of glowing remarks about who I was as a person and one little lie about them being scared of me on the twenty-fourth page was enough to put me away. I was shocked as coldness spread in my stomach that spread all over my body. I looked at my lawyer as the judge started to give me a bullshit motivational speech that she probably gave to hundreds of people she sentenced to prison.

"Be still," he said. "The judge is clearly torn at making this decision, she can suspend the sentence. It would go on your record but you wouldn't have to do the time."

"Mr. Alexander, you'll be turned over to the Department of Corrections immediately." She banged the gavel, got up, and walked away with her black robes swaying behind her.

Then I remembered Kerry had asked a lawyer what to say to put me away. Sure, we had a tumultuous relationship but I had not done anything to her for her to want me to go to prison. I was in this mess because she was cheating on me! I guess her lawyer gave her the right advice. I vowed never to see that evil woman again.

I had a house, a vehicle, homes under construction, a job, and a business – what would happen to all of that? Who was going to oversee or take of it? What will happen to my reputation now that I'm a convicted criminal?

Bailiffs came and handcuffed me while my lawyer hugged me and told me something I couldn't understand in my ear. They moved him away from me and, with my hands handcuffed behind my back, walked me to the holding cells on the lowest floor of the courthouse.

I stood in my new suit as a bailiff took the cuffs off me. In another ten seconds, I was going to be with the criminals that had also been sentenced, waiting to see what jail I would go to. The bailiff opened the door to the holding cell and I walked in thinking – *this is the end of Michael Alexander.*

IMPROVE YOUR PATH

12

INCARCERATED

I WAS DEVASTATED. I WAS ABLE TO MAKE A QUICK CALL TO my parents and they felt the same. The judge had made the decision; there was nothing to do but move forward with the new cards I had been dealt. I had many irons in the fire regarding work, property, and money, to which my brother and sister said they would step up and handle as much as they could.

My lawyer told me that based on how torn the judge was, I would be out on parole when I went up for it in April. "It's December. Just make it to April without getting into trouble and you'll celebrate Easter with your friends and family." Although it enlightened my heart to hear that, there was no way to deny that I was going to prison.

The next series of events were like a blur, as if I were in a dream. I went through the motions, almost as if it was happening to someone else. The first thing they did was board me in the Gray Goose, the slang term used for the big gray bus that transported inmates to and from the prison. I looked around and, oddly, felt safe because there were much smaller guys than me on the bus. If someone were to pick on anyone, I figured it would be one of the smaller guys. I had no way of basing that judgment, I just hoped to God I was right.

An officer handcuffed me next to a guy I had noticed as soon as I got on the bus because he had been talking to himself – loudly. Just my luck. I realized in 30 seconds the guy now handcuffed to me was a skitzo (a person with schizophrenia – a person who experiences delusions, hallucinations, incoherent speech, and illogical thinking).

In between the gibberish he was blabbing about, he would tell the guards he needed to take a shit. I guess he said it repeatedly because he got a big laugh the first time. He made a few motions of using the bathroom and somehow put me into his act. I was pissed. I wanted to either disappear or punch a hole through his mouth. However, I did my best yoga imitation and took deep breaths. I wasn't about to do anything to make me stay longer, especially since my lawyer was convinced I'd be out in a few months.

The guards yelled us out of the bus and we entered a facility with a big, open room. The ones who were there before and knew the drill started removing their clothes.

"Are you waiting for an invitation?" A guard yelled at me. "Strip you dumb motherfucker!"

Again, I was pissed. He had never said to strip in the first place! I held my tongue in check and removed my clothes. They formed us into a line and had us squish together. *I can't believe I'm actually writing this because of how degrading it was, but this was my life.* I had a guy's nut sack touching my backside and had butt cheeks smashed in front of me. They had us make a count and then split the group in half. I still don't know why they had to do that other than to degrade us. I stayed in the room with half of the men. A guard took out a massive spray gun, which I noticed as soon as we walked into the room. They ordered us to stay still and sprayed us with a nasty-smelling and lightly-stinging soapy spray. They said it was for lice. Had I had the choice, I would have rather they shaved my head!

We stood there with that 'spray' on our bodies for 45 minutes! Then they opened a door to the shower room, which consisted of eight showers with different water temperatures. We walked under each shower like a human car wash. I realized I would be treated as my prison number, not a person and not by my name. I had hit rock bottom.

After being dressed while still wet and unable to complain if the pants, boots, or shirt were too big or small, and after some other bullshit, I entered the prison.

I hadn't really talked to anyone else, but it didn't take a genius to realize that people got seriously hurt in there and nobody gave a fuck. I learned the rules early on, such as not asking anyone why they are there, not to stare at anyone, and probably most importantly, not to wake anyone up – if they were escaping prison with their dreams, there would be hell to pay if you brought them back to their real life.

I put on an I-don't-give-a-fuck persona. I had my mean face on, swore a lot, and talked like shit to everyone. Even still, I felt real inmates knew I was a first-timer. I occasionally thought of the partying, women, cars, and money I'd had, but I learned to stop thinking of those things because it just made matters worse.

I was put in a transfer facility, which means a temporary place to stay while a bed opened up in one of the jails. I got interviewed by a 75-year-old woman who saw right through my façade.

"Why are you here?"

I answered with an attitude. She reached out, grabbed my hands on the desk, and looked into my eyes.

"Don't act like this. I've been around these fools for over 40 years, and child, you are not like them. Don't let your time here change who you are."

My heart softened and I told her my story. I had been holding so much anger and frustration since I was sentenced that, being able to let it out, got me emotional.

"You're in a bad spot but you can't cry," she said. "If you cry here and they know it, they'll abuse or kill you. I'll hold you in here till your eyes aren't red."

I instantly composed myself, again doing my best deep-breathing yoga impersonation.

"I'm going to try to make sure you have a soft landing." She could tell by my look that I had no idea what she meant. "I'll try not to put you in a gladiator camp," she said as if I'd know what she meant. "Gladiator camps are the most dangerous. There's maybe one guard for every twenty inmates. Guards are heavily outnumbered there, so when there are fights, the guards usually don't interfere until the fight stops and fights there don't stop until someone is unconscious or worse. Texas gladiator camps are amongst the worst prisons in the country."

True to her word, I didn't get sent to a gladiator camp, but I still ended up in a shit hole. Most prisons are named after people, not the one I was sent to; it was named N-5. They didn't have cells for one or two people, it was more of a dorm setting – 28 convicts in one big room with tables in the middle.

First, I had to spend 30 days in segregation, called SEG, before joining the inmate population. There was no television and I could only shower every other day. A prisoner brought me my meals, but there was no interaction. I'm sure they have reasons for doing it that way, but it still doesn't make sense to me. It made me angrier of being there and more worried about what would happen to me. I had nothing better to do than imagine horrors and think how I would react if someone tried to punk me, who I should befriend, and many other questions I couldn't answer.

I had 30 days of thoughts and inevitably, I did some no-bullshit soul-searching. I was 30 years old. I thought about my life and the many opportunities I had squandered for having fun, sleeping with another woman, or trying to look cool. I came to a life-changing conclusion – I was there for what I had done. No one did it to me. I couldn't change the past but I could take full responsibility for what I did while I was there. I made a pact with myself that I would finally care for myself the way I should have. It was frightening because I had never had such little control of my life, yet it was motivational too because for the first time, I would make decisions based on a better, future me.

13

PRISON LIFE

CRAZY SHIT

Life in a Texas prison is brutal; it hardens the soul. So many crazy things happened I could write another book on just that.

I saw a 20-year-old kid go to a domino table and briefly talk to the four men playing. I was outside the glass so I couldn't hear what he said, but they quickly grabbed their things and left the table as he walked toward the staircase that would take him to the 3rd tier of the pod. I could hear them provoking him, but still not clear why. He reached the 3rd tier, put both hands on the top rail, and began climbing. It became clear to me.

"Hurry the fuck up," an inmate yelled coldly.

Another inmate followed with, "Make sure you hit the table!" and a few others laughed. These guys had been around and seen this before. But not me. I wanted to yell at the kid not to do it, he was so young, but there was nothing anyone could do.

To my surprise and horror, the kid dove face down into the table. I don't know what was happening to him that made him want to die, but unfortunately for him, he broke bones all over his body and lived for a few agonizing hours before finally passing. I found out later that he had a life sentence and had done as much of it as he could take, and believe me when I tell you, everyone's time in jail is different. This is just one tragic story of many that occur daily in places in prisons.

Fights are commonplace, most of them stemming from what to watch on TV. I learned early on that life on the inside is way different than on the outside. You can talk shit outside about fucking someone up yet the fight may never happen. If you say that on the inside, the guy you're talking to walks up to you and the fight gets going then and there. No one breaks it up, so it ends with someone really hurt or worse.

I think everyone has heard that you have to back your race there. It was true in my case. If you were Caucasian, you could have Black or Hispanic friends. That's not the issue. The issue would come if members of another race would jump a white guy and you were the only other white guy there. If you just saw it happen and didn't interfere, members of your own race would jump you. So if my Latino friend and some of his buddies jumped a white guy and I was the only other white guy there, I would have to fight my Latino friend or it would be twenty times worse. Every race did that. It's an unwritten law that, agree or disagree, you must abide by or things will not turn out well for you.

I met some of the worst people there. Liars, backstabbers (literally), bullshit artists, bullies, con men – you name it. Surprisingly, some of the worst people I met were Correctional Officers! Most don't talk to you; they talk at you – big difference. They have very little patience for the inmates. They certainly aid in making prison a pressure cooker at times. However, not all of them were assholes.

JAVIER

I met an amazing human being at the unit in West Texas – Javier Ontiveros – we're still great friends today. He was a Correctional Officer, but unlike many other COs, he talked to people respectfully and demanded they speak to him in the same manner. He was an intelligent man and a great conversationalist, something I was starving for. We would have regular conversations about everyday life, but my world was anything but normal, so it was so welcoming. I got a job working in the Officer's kitchen, so I'd see him 5-6 nights a week. Talking to him was the highlight of my days there.

Before getting to that unit, I was at a transfer unit in Abilene, TX. My lawyer had told me at the probation hearing when I was sentenced that if I kept out of trouble, there was no reason why I wouldn't be released. After only being at the unit for a few weeks, I saw the "parole board."

I pictured standing before a table full of people in suits, answering question after question. The reality was quite different. I walked into the room and saw one man who barely made eye contact. He explained that he would interview me and write a report that would be presented to the parole board. It seemed a little unfair, but I just continued with what I had rehearsed a dozen times in my head. I felt relieved when it was over. I had spoken the truth and waited for someone to tell me I qualified for parole. To my dismay, they didn't parole me. I had to wait another two years before being in front of the "board" again. Shit.

Now, I had been transferred to this unit in far West Texas, about 10 hours from home with the realization that I wouldn't even get the opportunity to see parole again for two more years. I wasn't savvy on these things, having never been in this kind of trouble before, so obviously, I had yet to learn why that was the decision. So, I asked Javier for some guidance.

"What did you say?" Javier asked me.

"The truth. I shouldn't be here in the first place. That son of a bitch tried to blackmail me. I let them know..."

"Hold up," he stopped me. "No wonder they didn't parole you. You didn't take responsibility for your actions."

"I told them the truth, though," I argued.

"You're not listening to me. They want to see that you've accepted responsibility for your actions, you're remorseful for what you've done, you've learned your lesson, and you'd never do anything like that again."

I promised myself when I was in that situation again, I would say the right thing.

So, I wasn't going home because I had blamed someone else for my actions. I realized that I needed to do a deep dive into who I was. I had to shut my ego up and see myself for who I really was, not who I thought I was or portrayed to others that I was. I needed to know why and how this could happen to me. I never considered myself to be perfect but I sure as hell wasn't a criminal. Why was I sentenced as one?

PROMISES MADE

I remembered the promises I made to myself, and immediately after, being that I wouldn't be let out anytime soon, I enrolled in every school program I could. I read everything I could get my hands on about improving or strengthening my mindset. I focused on self-improvement and human nature books. I needed to get to the core of what made me make the decisions that got me where I was.

After some time, I was asked to speak in some of the classes. So, I talked about how to function within our society, treat people, interact with people, and more about human behavior. Luckily, I was attending class and helping the teachers during the day and an officer's cook at night. That kept me out of many potential dangers and attached to some resemblance of normalcy.

Nine months in, an officer told me he needed to talk to me. I put down the ladle and expected the worst. "I'm sorry, Mike, but your father has cancer. As I understand it, he has the type with a 100% recurrence rate." My dad and I had never gotten along like a sitcom family, but still, he was my dad. Knowing he had cancer that he could beat but would come back again and again felt cruel. He was only 54 and had a lot more life to live. A few people had contacted me and sent me money, but I told them I'd appreciate it if they could send it to my dad instead. He could no longer work; however, thanks to my stepmother's good insurance, they could keep the lights on.

Javier asked me if I wanted to call him. After much thought, I decided against it. Dad wasn't going anywhere yet and we hadn't been on great terms when I was sent to prison.

I wanted to speak with him but was overwhelmed with guilt for not being there. I was afraid of getting emotional and wasn't at a place where crying was acceptable. It would be viewed as a sign of weakness, which meant you would be treated as such until you proved otherwise. I was also still discovering myself and wanted to say things to him that I hadn't quite figured out yet. "I think I need more time, but thanks for the offer."

Even though I didn't get to see the actual outside world, I didn't care to see even the inside of the outside world, meaning I didn't go outside for a year. It ripped my heart to look out and see traffic pass by, regular people living their lives with all the freedoms of the world while my time was regulated and confined. It was easier for me not even to see the daylight. I focused on learning, teaching, and staying alive.

I got word after 19 months that I was getting transferred. I hoped against hope that it meant I was getting out, but no such luck. Instead, they sent me to a prison in far east Texas. Tennessee Colony, TX, to be exact. This was at least good news because it brought me only 2 hours from home. The place I was in, West Texas, was so far from where I was from I hadn't received a single visitor.

SOUL-LESS

I met a 60-year-old lifer, a convicted murderer since he was in his 20s. One day, he kept looking at me and started a conversation.

"You look like you have questions," he said as he looked at me through his black horn-rimmed glasses.

"No, I'm good," I answered. I had already learned that you don't ask people questions about why they're in jail. But that doesn't mean that you aren't sometimes curious. And, I'd heard that he was in for murder.

"Come on, boy, let it out. It's okay."

I got closer and asked the question that had been burning in my mind since I met him. I was a little worried about how he'd react, but I was being transferred in a day or so, so I asked, "Are you really in here for murder?"

He answered by holding up four fingers, meaning he had killed four people. That answer shocked me because he did not look like what I, and probably most people, picture as a murderer – and he had done it four times. He was well spoken, kept to himself, stayed extremely fit, and had a job in prison, which meant he was a hard worker.

"What does it feel like to actually kill someone? I mean, how did you feel after?"

He nodded as if he knew that was the question I wanted to ask. "I said it was okay for you to ask, so I'll answer. The people I killed deserved to die, and I didn't feel shit once I killed them." He lifted his coffee cup. "See this cup, I like it, it serves a purpose, but it don't have a soul. I could smash it to pieces and wouldn't feel any way about it. That's the same way I feel about you. I wouldn't feel any way if I killed you or that feller there, that feller there, and everyone else. You're all like things to me. As long as we are respectful here, there will be no problems. If not, I'll kill someone again. Murder is natural." He said it so matter-of-factly that it made me shiver.

14

THE BRACELET

FIGHTING STANCE

Before I got transferred, some of the cool guards got me a gift. Well, they couldn't give it to me, but they showed it to me and then sent it to Debra's address. It was a bracelet.

"You got in here for fighting," Javier said. "Are you left-handed or right-handed?"

"Right, but I fight left-handed," I answered.

He got in a fighting stance like a left-handed person would fight: with the right hand closer to the opponent and in front of your face. "I want you to put this bracelet on your right hand when you get out. That way, if you're ever in a situation where you're about to fight on the outside, you'll see the bracelet in front of your face. I want it to remind you of your time in prison and realize that whatever reason you're about to fight, it's not worth it. Find a way out."

I didn't know what to say except a heartfelt and sincere thank you. I almost let out a tear but held it in.

FIGHT! FIGHT! FIGHT!

Now that I'm on the topic of fighting, I did get into a couple of them. I had some pictures sent in of me with some UFC fighters taken at the after-party of Brad Imes's TUF Season 2 Finale against Rashad Evans. Those who saw them assumed I was a professional fighter. As I had mentioned, people don't ask too many questions about your outside life in prison and if they do, all you had to say was you didn't want to talk about it and the matter gets dropped. So when people would ask me if I was a professional fighter, I'd mumble menacingly, "I don't want to talk about it."

I would work at night, get out at 5 AM, go work out – 1,000 pushups and 500 box jumps, be in the dorm before shift change at 6 AM, sleep till lunch, go to school, and work again at 9 PM – rinse and repeat.

So, I would sleep during the day. This was when I was staying in a large room, barracks-style with 27 other inmates. Most people were respectful when other inmates were asleep. Sleep was sacred. No one wanted to be yanked out of a dream back to the shitty reality we were all in. When someone was sleeping, out of respect, people playing dominos would put a blanket over the table because, apparently, you're not playing dominos correctly if you're not slapping the shit out of the table. Yet, for some reason, this guy wanted to try me. He would walk by me when I was sleeping and scream so I'd wake up. I would be groggy and not know who the jerk was that kept doing that because he'd scream and scurry away. I had my suspicions but no one there wanted to rat anyone out, so I didn't approach him without proof.

One day, he was in a domino game about five feet away from my bed, which was much closer than it had ever been. In classic asshole style, they didn't have a blanket on the table, so I woke up to hard slaps a few feet away from me. I got off my bed and asked them if they could please put a blanket on the table. "I only need a couple hours more of sleep."

"Sure, bro. I got you." He said with a smile.

I jumped back into my bed, and not more than ten minutes later, he slapped the table and yelled something.

I got out of bed again and he threw a domino that hit my face in front of everybody. Oh shit. What do I do now?

I was torn about fighting because I had been doing a lot of self-exploration and examination. I had been practicing letting things go and not bother me, which got noticed and led me to be a teacher's assistant. However, the moment was upon me – he had blatantly disrespected me and hit me in the face with a domino. If I did nothing, my daily life would go from bad to worse really quickly. The thing about prison is nobody really WANTS to fight, but everyone in there WILL fight, especially when they've been disrespected.

Usually, when there's a planned fight, the fighters wrap their hands so people don't get nicked and cut up and have to explain anything to the guards. However, there was no time for that. We squared up and I kicked his ass quite handily.

We swung at each other a few times; his punches missed or grazed while mine located and popped. I knocked him down and, in classic jail-fight style, the inmates picked him up. He tried to wrestle me but had no technique. The fact that he was about six inches taller did nothing to help in the wrestling department because I was about fifty pounds heavier. I got him off me, punched him square in the jaw, and knocked him out.

"All I wanted to do was get some fucking sleep!" I yelled at his comatose ass.

I figured the issue was over but I was wrong. He was a black guy and I'm a white guy. His face was cut and I had almost broken his jaw so it was bruised. The head black guy talked to the head white guy to settle how to squash the beef. They felt it right that I bring him his food for a week because he was woozy and banged up. However, the main reason was that if the wrong guard saw his cut face and started an investigation, we would both be in trouble. I just wanted it to be over. At first, he didn't eat the food, thinking I had put something in it, and refused the "deal." That is, until the head black guy forced him to take it—jail justice at its finest.

BEWARE THE CORRECTIONAL OFFICERS

Inmates weren't the only people fucking each other up. I never got too much into the politics of jail, but some crazy shit would happen. I was with another inmate being escorted by two guards somewhere and we turned a corner and walked into a blind spot - where the cameras couldn't see you. One of the guards told me to look down, so I stared at my feet. Both guards proceeded to fuck up the other inmate. When they were done, he was slumped on the ground, no doubt bleeding profusely. I wouldn't know, though; I was staring at my feet.

"What did you see?" A guard asked me.

"Nothing," I answered.

"Who are you with?"

"Nobody,"

"Good. Get the fuck to where you have to go."

DAD AND I HAVE THE TALK

Once I transferred to The Michael Unit in Tennessee Colony, I was at the trusty camp outside the walls of the main unit. I got a job working for the warden. I was deep in my self-improvement journey and felt ready to have an honest conversation with my dad.

He walked right up to me but I didn't recognize him until he stopped in front of me. My father was 6 ft, 200 pounds when I last saw him. This shell of a man was 5'9 and weighed 135 pounds soaking wet. He had undergone a lot of radiation and chemo, including surgery where they removed part of his esophagus and stomach. We hugged and began chit-chatting.

"Do you know when you're getting out?" He asked.

"No, I could do the entire four years."

"Well, whenever you get out, know you can stay with me. Although I can't work, my company is still afloat, so you have employment there if you want."

I had written down the harsh things I would say to him. Even though I felt terrible for him because of what he was going through, I had to keep the word I made to myself to have this conversation with him the next time I saw him.

"Dad, I've had a lot of time to think and concluded that I let myself down, but not anymore. I'm making changes when I get out. Actually, I already started making changes in my mindset. I no longer think the same. When I leave here, I'm going all out on my dreams and will never be told again about my "potential." Listen, please, this is important. If you don't support my goals, I will cut you out. We'll never talk again. You don't have to go out of your way to help me, but don't give me any negativity."

He thought for a moment and answered in a classic fatherly fashion. "We'll see who you are when you get out. If you start partying and girl-chasing, this conversation ain't gonna mean much."

The guard let the visit go longer than what was allowed, which helped my dad and me to have a very meaningful conversation. By the time he left, we had buried much of the bad blood that had marked our relationship since I was a teenager.

I thought I had hundreds of friends before going to prison. I would say 'what's up' and wave to many "friends" when hanging out. Most people who knew me certainly thought I was popular. It hurt my feelings when I realized out of all of my so-called friends, only two people wrote me consistently: Brad Imes – a UFC fighter, and Debra Goodman. My sister also wrote me regularly but she's a sister. Brad told his sponsors at Warrior Wear I was a great athlete who had a rough childhood and was making up for my mistakes but that they should sponsor me when I got out. Just like that, Warrior Wear sent a truckload of gear to my house. It was there waiting when I was released!

I had hardly gone outside in the other prisons, but we had more freedoms in that camp, so I was always out. The highlights were when we would play softball games against local churches. It always felt good to interact with normal people with kind enough hearts to spend a Saturday with a bunch of convicts. Plus, it was softball! We had bats! I couldn't imagine if some of the inmates I met in other prisons were given bats. It was like being in the nicest place in hell!

PAROLE BOARD # 2

Not long after, I got word that I was to go in front of the parole board again. Being that I worked for the warden, we had some conversations. He was a firm believer that I did not belong in prison. Like many others, he felt the punishment did not fit the crime. I asked him for advice and then went through the trouble of listening to my previous parole hearing.

He echoed what Javier had told me, "Ya, don't do what you did last time. They know you've cooked, taught other inmates, and kept your nose clean, so you don't have to tell them much of that. Just ensure you take personal responsibility for the actions that brought you here."

I wasn't overly optimistic since I only had about 18 months left on my sentence. I figured I would just be here, finish my time and be ready to start over once my sentence was fulfilled. The truth was, at that point, I was fine with that. Was I even ready for home?

I did precisely what Javier and the warden told me to do in my parole hearing, which, just like before, was one man writing a report to be presented to the parole board. The parole board representative tried to trip me up a little when he asked me what happened outside my control that got me here. I didn't know if he was referring to the fact that I was being blackmailed but either way, I didn't mention it. "I would have never been in any of the bad situations I found myself in if I had used better judgment and exercised more self-control."

I was granted parole and released on June 3, 2009 - two months after the interview. I swore to never, ever do anything that would strip me of my freedom again. Something within me had shifted. I was different.

I'll never forget when I got to put on the bracelet Javier and other correctional officers gave me. I put up my fists and it shined in front of me. I had spent 962 days in a place where I couldn't cry. I was a free man who fulfilled his obligation to the state and was ready to keep every promise I made to myself. I looked at the bracelet, not my fists.

Standing alone in a room, full of gratitude and optimism, I was able to be me and let out my emotions. I cried.

"World, I'm ready."

15

FREE, BUT BROKE

FREEDOM; YOU'RE NOT WHO I THOUGHT YOU WERE

NO ONE TOLD ME MUCH ABOUT MY BELONGINGS WHILE I WAS in jail. I had a hunch I'd probably lose the house. After all, we were a hard-working family, but not exactly the Rockefellers. I didn't expect family members to pay my mortgage for a long time. The worst news was that my dad had cancer, which was bad enough. Still, the only thing on my mind was getting the hell out of the walls that had trapped me for far too long.

My sister Joni, Coty, my little brother, and one of Joni's friends came to pick me up. I was happy to see them; however, the prison released me wearing what I called a clown suit! I wore a stupid shirt, yellow pants, and some Bruce Lee slippers. I felt ridiculous. I told her to pull into the next gas station or any parking area so I could get some of my clothes on.

Joni stopped in the first place she could, went to the trunk, and handed me some raggedy shorts, a t-shirt I used to work out in, and flip-flops!

"Out of all my clothes, this is what you bring me the day I get out of jail?"

"We were running a little late. It's the first thing I saw so I just grabbed it." She said.

It felt like a glass of cold water spilled down my back. I knew something wasn't right. "It's okay, I'm not mad. I'm happy as hell to see you. But, tell me the truth, how bad is it for me?"

"Well, you're gonna find out when we get to Dad's anyway." She sighed. "We weren't able to keep your house."

"Okay, I was kind of expecting that. What about my truck?"

"We couldn't keep that either." She answered.

"That sucks. What about my clothes?"

"I'm so sorry, Mike. It's kinda my fault." She said softly. "I was dating a guy and we were about to go out but he didn't have the right clothes, so he asked if he could wear something of yours. I knew you probably wouldn't have cared so I said okay. He kept burrowing them as time passed, but I wasn't on top of it and didn't realize he never brought anything back. I never really thought about your clothes till today. I couldn't believe it, it's all gone."

I took a deep breath. I had just gotten out of prison and didn't want to ruin my first hour with a fight over clothes. "I get it. I had like, umm, maybe thirty pairs of sneakers and shoes..."

"Those are gone too." She said.

"Give me a minute?" I asked. She apologized again and got back in the car. I didn't know how to feel. I was out of jail. I was happy. Yet, the realization hit me like a slow bullet; *I don't have shit to my name!* I only had the fifty-dollar check the prison gives inmates when they release them. It was such a strange sensation to feel relief, sadness, joy, and fear for the future all at once. I did the only thing I could: I took a deep breath and got back in the car.

"What do you want to eat?" Joni asked.

I only had fifty bucks to my name. "I don't know," I saw a Subway coming up ahead, "there's a Subway."

They pretty much left me alone to my thoughts as we ate. I had only been out for an hour and life had already punched me in the stomach. I had money, no cars, no house, and no businesses; that's how people knew me. Now was everyone going to see me as a broke felon? A thought came to me that strengthened the resolve I had been cultivating while in prison. *If I got nothing, then I got nothing to lose! Fuck it.*

I wasted no time. I got released on June 3, 2009, and started working for my father on June 8. Brad Imes, the great friend and MMA fighter, set me up to start training mixed martial arts the following week. I had rehearsed what I would say to the MMA coach repeatedly in my head and out loud countless times in prison. Luckily, Rudy, an old high school friend, gave me a ride and sat in on the interview.

The moment came when I met my coach, Travis Lutter, a highly decorated and well-known figure in the MMA community. He was a legend in the making and I would have considered it a true honor if he trained me.

"Coach, I know you know what happened to me and where I just came out of. All I ask is not to judge me for my past and to get to know who I really am. For my part, I promise to be the best student you've ever had. Please, give me a chance."

Travis smiled. "Mike, I hope this comes out the right way. It sucks what you went through, but I really don't care. I'm much more interested in your goals."

"I want to fight," I said, looking him in the eye so he took me seriously.

"How soon?"

"I was thinking in three months," I answered.

This time, he laughed but saw I was serious and stopped. "Wait. What? No one does that. Mike, no one but trained killers get in cages to fight. Most of them have been fighting their entire lives or at least a decade. How about we temper those expectations and get some training and we'll play it by ear?"

In true Rudy fashion, he busted my balls on the way home. "Great job, Mike, Travis was really impressed with you!" His sarcasm was on point.

"I saw that going better in my head," I admitted. "Your right, I don't think he cared for me much." We both laughed but my goal didn't change, I still wanted to fight in three months.

Shortly after that, my cousin Molly and her husband, a chiropractor, came to the house. I was outside and found it odd that they came in two vehicles. We hugged and caught up, and then he said, "So listen, Mike. We want to help you get on your feet. We have this 2002 Dodge Dakota," he motioned to the blue truck he came in on, "we'll sell it to you for twenty-five hundred."

"Jason, I appreciate it, man but I don't have twenty-five hundred lying around," I said.

"Oh no, I get it. As I said, we want to help you out. Take the truck and make payments to us whenever you can."

"How big are the payments?"

"Whenever you can and however you can. How's that?"

"That's pretty fucking good man, thank you! But... are you sure?" Thankfully, they were.

My older brother Jason had bought me a good pair of shoes, and I was still wearing my father's clothes, but someone had trusted me with a truck and I was laser-focused on paying what I owed as soon as possible. I was laying rock for my dad's company, leaving at three to shower, jumping in my Dodge Dakota, which I was pleased to find out was a V-8, driving to Fort Worth, and training. I did that every day, seven days a week. I had three promises to keep:

- To be Travis' best student.
- To pay off the truck.
- To keep the promise to myself of manifesting the potential people had said I had my entire life, which was the most important.

HER

My schedule had me working and training every day. I had received many calls and texts from friends to swing by one of the old hangout joints for drinks. I turned them all down nicely. It just wasn't my scene. Besides getting me laid a lot, all it really got me was to blow money, meet the wrong women, and get my ass thrown in prison. I was all set.

One day, my friend Rudy convinced me to swing by and say hello to friends who had been asking about me. The place they were going had an outside bar and I could say hi to them without ever walking in. I agreed, "Okay, I'll go. But I'm staying outside, on the sidewalk. Don't try to talk me into going in."

I went and saw a bunch of friends and acquaintances. I thought the "old me" would get thirsty for that life again but it didn't; like I said, I was laser-focused. One of the girls there was Jennifer, a girl I had known before and asked out several times but never went out with me because I was too wild. We would hang out but never dated.

Rudy had told her what had happened to me, and her friend Micah and she had cried for me. "I couldn't believe you would ever be in a place like that. It felt so unfair." We ended the night with her offering me her number. I had wanted to date this girl for years, but at that point I just slumped my shoulders as if in defeat.

"Look, I don't want you to have any false expectations. I don't have much. I'm scared to death of even being here, so I don't know what we'd do. Besides, I can't even afford to take you to a nice dinner."

She looked at me with a twinkle in her eye and a smirk. "Got it. I don't care about any of that. I'm not offering a marriage proposal; take my phone number and call me from time to time."

I called her the next day and we talked for an hour. I called her the next day after that, the next after that, and the next after that – rinse and repeat. That became how I used my newly found freedom; work, bust my ass at the gym, talk to Jen, and sleep happily exhausted. Everything was going great, the only problem was, I really wanted to fight but my coach kept telling me I wasn't ready. I still thought differently.

16

NORMALCY AND FIGHTING

LOVE AND WORK

THINGS STARTED GETTING TO NORMAL WHEN MY DAD SAID he'd let me sell jobs, and we could split the difference between whatever I charged over what he usually got. I started doing that and picked up some great-paying jobs on weekends. I was such a good salesperson that we'd make more on weekends than weekdays.

I assumed everyone would think I would return to the 'old Mike' once I had money. The truth was, I was happy with my boring life. I didn't have to be the king of attention. I was more than content to work, make money, go all out in the gym, and talk to Jen at night.

Before I continue, I must say that Jennifer was a brilliant woman. She has a doctorate in Educational Leadership and was an Autism Specialist. I say that so I wouldn't feel bad telling you that we would watch Jeopardy together while on the phone and she would always get many more answers right. I never admitted this to her, but the only times I'd beat her was when it would rain in the afternoons. See, they first aired the show at 2 p.m. and then at night. I could never see the 2 p.m. show though, unless it rained because we couldn't work. All she knew was that on some days, I had strokes of genius!

We went on our first date on September 6. I fell in love. I had never had a relationship of that caliber before. She didn't care about money or that I was in a rebuilding phase. She supported me and built me up whenever she felt I needed it. She was my best friend. I had never experienced unconditional love and friendship at that level up to that point. She meant the world to me. She added another reason I wanted to succeed so badly.

I was in a constant state of trying to impress her, although she had no requirements for me to meet. The only thing she asked was that I be good to her and treat her right. Those were her requirements, and I met them in every way, every day, no exceptions.

After we had been dating for a few months, she called her uncle, who was the Vice President of a commercial construction company and told him all about me. He met with me out of respect for her but said he hired me as a supervisor out of what he saw in me.

The only problem was that the position required a lot of travel. Having gone through miscommunication with my probation officers in the past that eventually led me to prison, I ran it by my current P.O. before I took the position. He knew I was a no-nonsense, hard-working guy and told me it was okay as long as I checked in every month when I had to. I made him put it in writing and then accepted the offer.

I began traveling to Alabama, Jacksonville, the Keys, and all over the East Coast since we did many jobs for the Coast Guard. I even went to Venice, Louisiana, where the famous BP Oil Spill occurred. Without exception, every town I found myself in I would find a place to train. Every day.

MY FIRST FIGHT

Unbeknownst to my coaches, I had started making phone calls to promoters, trying to sell them on letting me fight. I felt more than ready. I had a strong desire for two things: to prove myself in the cage and to see if I loved fighting. I knew I loved the training, but I was wasting my time if I didn't love the actual fighting. I had to know. One promoter told me he would put me on his card. I was ecstatic but nervous to tell Travis and the coaching staff that had poured so much into me.

"I told you, you should train for at least a year before your first fight." Travis countered when I told him. "People at this level have been doing it for all their lives. You'll get killed getting in there too soon."

"I hear you, but I'm going all out, giving you every ounce of energy and strength I have. I need to do this, coach."

"You're a grown-ass man, Mike. If you want to fight that badly, I won't stop you. However, you will not wear my colors."

That hit me like a gut punch. Part of why I wanted to fight was to make him and the gym proud. "What?"

"You will not fly my flag. I can't stop you from fighting, but I can stop you from wearing my logo. Also, I won't go to the fight because I don't condone it. However, I do like you and see you working your ass off, so I'll send one of our coaches to be there with you."

The day came, October 3, 2009, and I was waiting for my music to hit and walk out from the hallway and enter the arena. I had requested to be on the first fight on the card. I wanted to get it over with without watching any other fights. A myriad of different emotions came at me at once. I was almost on the verge of tears because this fight was the first thing I had accomplished of the many things I told myself I'd do when in prison. I had warmed up, but waiting in that hallway, with a tsunami of nervous energy coursing through my body, my sweat had dried off and I got cold. I told my coach, and he took out his mitts, and I started hitting the pads as I waited for my music.

I had walked out of prison weighing 212 pounds. When my music played, Simple Man, by Lynyrd Skynyrd, I walked out a lean, muscular 170 pounds. Even though I was scared shitless, I was also very proud of myself.

I was ready.

I was a white belt with three months of training and no striking experience. Unfortunately, my opponent, Arturo Flores, a purple belt in Jiu Jitsu and a black belt in Kung Fu, was good at everything. The only way my team saw me having a shot was to take him down and do some ground and pound, which means wrestling him to the ground and rain down punches and elbows on him. A flood of memories washed over me as the announcer introduced me. Both fighters were called to the center of the ring, given instructions, looked each other in the eye, tapped gloves, and returned to their 'corners.'

It was go time.

I came out a little faster than Arturo after the sound of the bell. We danced around each other, throwing jabs in the air, trying to find our range. We feinted punches, seeing how the other would react if we really threw one. Nothing mattered but Arturo Flores. I wasn't thinking about prison, the time the Swede almost killed herself, the guy I punched so hard I lost my freedom, or that I had started talking to a fantastic woman. Nothing mattered but the man in front of me who was there to inflict terrible pain on me.

I saw an opening and got close to him and took him down to the mat. I was on top of him but he didn't panic. He was waiting for me to make a mistake and reverse the position or get back up. Unfortunately for him, all I had trained for was to control him on the ground and throw blows. I did just that. I punched him everywhere: his face, his ribs, his ears, and every other legal place. The three-minute round seemed to last forever. I looked at the referee several times, wondering why he hadn't stopped the fight. Arturo was bleeding badly, and I also felt that I had loosened a tooth or two. That guy was one tough son of a bitch. Amazingly, the round ended. I popped up, sweating profusely but fresh as a daisy, and went to my corner.

My coach nearly hugged me. "You're doing exactly what we need you to do. He's all fucked up. He wobbled to his corner and is bleeding pretty badly. Now listen, two words, relentless pressure..."

Round 2.

Arturo came out a lot more weary and cautious. He knew he had a striking advantage so he tried to move around and pop me with jabs and one-twos. Just like in the first round, he overextended a jab and I did a level-change and took him back down to the mat. I began beating him badly, as I did in the first round. I was so focused on hitting him that I hadn't noticed he 'walked' up the fence with his feet. I swung down hard and missed, and in an instant, he pushed off the fence and turned his body while grabbing my left arm.

Before I knew it, we were both lying on our chests, but my left arm was underneath him. I knew what he wanted to do so I tried to pull my arm out as hard as I could but had no leverage. He got me in a belly-down armbar, and a pain accompanied by a flash of white light hit me. He was about to break my arm so I tapped on the mat with my other hand. I had lost!

I didn't know how to feel when the referee raised his arm in victory. I hadn't sustained any damage other than the momentary pain of the armbar. I thought I did great, but still, I lost.

After the referee let his arm go, I took the two steps toward him and told him, "Great fight." It's a sign of respect most fighters give the winner.

He looked at me and I saw the damage I had done to his face. "I'm pretty sure you broke an orbital," He motioned to his entire face, "It's not good."

"Ya, but you won," I said

"I don't know about that."

We hugged again - he went to the emergency room - I went to the after-party.

Everyone at the gym clapped for me when I arrived the following Monday. A few of my teammates had gone to see the fight, maybe hoping to watch me get my cocky ass kicked. Either way, they gave everyone an accurate account of the fight. Even the promoter couldn't believe I had only been training for three months and performed the way I did.

Travis called me into his office. "I heard all about your fight. Congratulations."

"Thanks, coach. But I lost."

"Arturo is an experienced martial artist, and you beat his ass, regardless of what the records say. I appreciate you fighting the way you did. I called you in here to let you know that it would be an honor for me if the next time you fight, you wear my colors."

"Thanks, coach. I can't wait to get in there again and get this L off me."

"Ya, about that," he said. "You're about to turn 34. You don't have time to absorb many more losses. Do me a favor; promise me you'll give me a year to properly train you before you fight again."

"You got it, coach, I promise."

"Good. Now, get out there and loosen up. We got work to do."

17

LIFE GETS BETTER – THE END OF MY MMA CAREER

MALEX ENTERPRISE

Jennifer and I were on a roll. I worked for her uncle, so I was *in* with her family. I had lost my first fight but felt like I had won it, and I was training almost every day, no matter where I was, but the problem was, I was traveling too often. At around the six-month mark, she gave me an ultimatum: she didn't want to be with someone who was hardly ever there. While I was enjoying my job, I couldn't argue with her. I had traveled often in other jobs and knew how easy it was to have to find trouble. We were very happy together, so she wanted to eliminate any chance of that happening to her, as it did in her first marriage.

I was in Jacksonville, Florida, when I called her uncle, my boss, and told him I had to resign. "I appreciate the opportunity, sir, but quite frankly, I'm not going to lose your niece, the woman I love, to a job." He understood and allowed me to leave on good terms, which came in handy later.

I drove 16 hours straight from Jacksonville to Fort Worth. I entered the house, went to the bedroom, and scared the hell out of Jennifer when I flipped on the light.

"I'm here, babe, for good."

She rubbed the sleep away from her eyes. "What do you mean? What happened? Did you get fired?"

"No! I told your uncle I had to resign and he understood." I said as I sat on the bed while she propped herself up on pillows.

"Why?" she asked softly. "You loved working there."

"You said you wouldn't deal with all the travel, and as much as I like working for your uncle, being with you is more important. Besides, I've worked on construction projects for years; I know them from front to back and everywhere in between. I've always had an entrepreneurial spirit. I'll start my own General Contracting company.

I figured I'd find a good job quickly, but very few projects were going on that needed my skillset. I put some feelers out there and got a call to be the night Superintendent for a remodel of a Wal-Mart Supercenter. With no other prospects to choose from, I accepted the position. I told her uncle, my recent employer, about the opportunity.

"Well, you did great here. I tell you what, I'll hire you on a contract basis; you can do the work or sub it out if you want."

That's how my company, Malex Enterprise LLC, (named from the first initial of my first name and the first four letters of my last name), was born. Most good things take time to build, and this was no different. We started making just $2,000 a month, then $10,000, then $25,000. While the company grew, Jen was also promoted to Director of Special Education. The dreams we had were beginning to become our reality.

Life was good. The only thing nagging me was the L on my fight record.

FIGHT DAY

My 2nd fight was on August 7, 2010. I was true to my word with my coach, Travis Lutter, and trained for almost a year. I first got to the gym as a gifted athlete willing to outwork everyone, but I was very green; I didn't know shit about how to fight properly. By the time August 7 rolled in, I had acquired some fighting skills. I had practiced striking six and seven days a week and had earned a Blue Belt in Jiu Jitsu. (Today, as a seasoned black belt, this line made me giggle a bit.)

I couldn't wait for the fight, not only to test myself and get a win but also because there was a lot of trash-talking coming from my opponent, Donnie Bedore. My coach, Travis Lutter, was the first American-born Black Belt awarded by Carlos Machado, a pioneer in bringing jiu jitsu to America and a legend in the sport. Travis went on to win the Ultimate Fighter 4 show and fought for the Middleweight championship in the UFC, mainly depending on his unmatched Jiu-Jitsu and wrestling.

Since we were known as a strong Jiu-Jitsu gym, Donnie had said, "They think they're the best at Jiu-Jitsu. Not only will I beat Mike Alexander, I will beat them at their own game and submit him." Talk like that is common before the fights to create more awareness and hype. Needless to say, everyone at the gym told me I better not lose that fight!

Fight Day came and I was ready. The fights were held in a rodeo arena, in a metal building in the Texas August heat – it was hotter than hell in that building! Travis told me to go for the win. "If you can stop him, stop him. Don't play around looking for a submission." Still, my dumbass entered the cage looking for the submission.

The bell rang and Round 1 began. I moved around, looking for a take-down more than throwing many meaningful punches. It was as if I hadn't practiced striking for a year because I didn't throw much. The bell rang and my corner told me I played around too much and most likely lost the round. I glanced at the people in the crowd: Dad, Mom, Jen, my step kids, cousins, other family members, fellow gym fighters, and friends. There was no way I was going to lose to that guy. Not in front of all of them. I came out for Round 2 on a mission to just fight.

Donnie felt my power and didn't initiate much after that. I kept being the aggressor and easily won the second round. "We're one and one!" My coach said, "Don't leave it in the hands of the judges. Take his ass out!"

The bell for Round 3 sounded, and I kept pressuring him. I finally got him in a clinch and, after a scramble, ended up on his back. I was in a prime position to choke him out, which is what I wanted to do all along. I sat atop his back and used my legs to flatten his legs out, (so he was in a prone position). I rained punches on his face and head but he kept his hands up, protecting himself as best as he could, even though he couldn't improve his position.

I kept looking at the ref, Jake Montalvo, to see if he would stop the fight. Jake came near and I stopped punching, thinking it would be stopped because I didn't want it to stop by punches; I wanted the fucking submission. However, Donnie has his own pride – he didn't want to be choked out after talking all that shit.

I glanced at my corner, and they yelled at me to end the fight. "Fuck it," I muttered and threw a barrage of punches until Jake pulled me off of Donnie. I won by a Technical Knock Out (TKO)!

I pushed myself off him and jumped up, feeling absolutely on fire. I ran to the side of the cage where my fans were and straddled the cage. It was an incredible feeling to be locked in the cage with a trained fighter, compete my ass off, and win in front of the people closest to me. I screamed like a wild man, flexed, and punched my chest while the crowd cheered loudly. I had always wondered what a moment like that would feel like. It was surreal. I'll never forget it. Seeing their faces and hearing their screams was more than I had hoped for.

KIDNEY TROUBLE

After that, Travis started lining up fights for me. The problem was that the fighters would back out one after another before the fight. This up and down messed with my body because I would typically weigh around 200 pounds, then I'd cut weight to 180, only to not have the fight and get back to 200, to then get another fight and cut weight to 180 again, only to not have that fight fall through. Usually, fighters go up and down in weight twice to three times a year; I did it every month! The weight fluctuation didn't sit well with my 35-year-old body. Still, training was going well and I was ready to stack up more opponents. I felt good and was ready to take on all comers at this point. Until it happened.

While training at my home gym, my partner asked if I felt okay.

"Sure man, why?"

"I don't know, and I don't mean this in a bad way, but you don't feel as strong as usual. You feel pretty weak."

I could barely move ten minutes later. I was rushed to the emergency room and later told I had rhabdomyolysis. I'm not sure of its technical definition, but I was told, in layperson's terms, that due to the heavy training, my cardiac and skeletal muscles were secreting an enzyme that was intoxicating my kidneys. I was told that if I tried to cut weight again, I would most likely get so sick and never be able to cut weight again. Since MMA is a licensed sport that requires medical clearance to fight, cutting weight again might have made me so sick that I would never be able to cut again, which meant no more fighting. Just like that, my MMA career was over.

Never to be beaten by bad news, Travis told me, "Hey, you're leaving MMA. But let's face it, at your age, you were never going to the UFC. How about we solely focus on Jiu-Jitsu? What do you say?"

What could I say? If I wanted to compete, I didn't have a choice.

"Okay, coach. But know this: I don't care how old I am, I'm not training to stay in shape. If I focus on just Jiu Jitsu, it's to be a World Champion."

Travis laughed and just said "Good." He is a man of few words.

Dear reader, I want to come full circle with you. In chapter 2, I shared about my first few matches of the IBJJF No Gi World Championships. I stopped when I mentioned I had made it to the finals. If you're interested in knowing how I did, I'll tell you – I went on to win in 20 seconds by submission for my first world championship!

11 months later, I won my 2nd world championship, this time at Brown Belt.

After six years of training, almost to the day, I earned my Black Belt from Travis – the date was June 12, 2015.

Through hard work, consistency, and dedication, I accomplished every Jiu-Jitsu goal I aspired to.

18

DIVORCE

DREAM JOB OR NIGHTMARE?

I THINK MOST FANS IN THE WORLD ONLY THINK OF professional athletes as only competing in their sport. We don't think of vicious NFL linemen picking up their daughters from elementary school and taking them out for ice cream. News flash – when the sport is over, life goes on. My brief MMA career was over and my professional Jiu-Jitsu career was over, but life continued.

Jennifer and I had sold our giant house – it was too much house; her kids were in college and it was just us two and her mother who stayed in the smaller one by the pool. I had built the house and we had so much equity in it that everything made sense for us to sell. We all moved into a smaller home we rented while I built a smaller one than we had on more land.

Jen and I were on a roll. I could wear whatever, including a pink shirt and she would like it. We never argued. We split the finances responsibly, with no one controlling the money. Life was beautiful.

About ¾ of the way done building a beautiful, modern farmhouse, Jen got a call to apply for the Deputy Commission or Education for the

Texas Education Agency. That was her dream job. It's equivalent to a G-League player getting a call from an NBA team or an AAA baseball player getting a call from an MLB team. The problem was that if she got the job, she would have to be out of town on weekdays and we would see each other only on weekends – not an ideal situation for a marriage.

I was torn. She had made me promise not to travel as much, which I kept. I stopped traveling. I didn't even go out on Guys-Night if she didn't come with me, which, thankfully, the guys didn't mind. When travel was absolutely necessary, I would fly back in two days to be home for a few days and fly back out. Gone were the days when I'd be out of the house for more than a week. My commitment to her made our relationship incredible; we were each other's best friends. I did not want anything interfering with how we were.

On the other hand, this was the big league calling for her. Would she resent me if I opposed it?

"Michael, this is my dream job. It allows me to help the most kids at once, and you know that's my passion."

I remembered many conversations with her telling me of her reminding teachers that their top priority had to be the kids. Somehow, I tried to tell her I supported her but felt uneasy about what it could do to us.

"You know what? We don't have to make the decision now. I have yet to interview, let alone get the job. Besides, they have a ton of qualified candidates. Let's see if they even offer me the job before we decide anything. It would be silly to discuss such an intense conversation if it can't happen anyway."

I agreed to table that topic of conversation unless it became unavoidable. She interviewed once and killed it. She went again and did even better! I received the news of her being offered her dream job with mixed emotions. It was time to address the elephant in the room.

"If you take it, what would it mean to our daily lives?" Our coffees were on the kitchen table and we sat across each other, not as rivals, as two people who loved each other but had a hard choice to make. The position came with a significant raise for her but it wasn't as if we were hurting for money, so the finances were a very small part of the equation.

"Well, I supported you when you traveled..."

"Until you asked me not to travel anymore." I interrupted.

She paused. "Yes. I acknowledge that and still love you for that. But I think you'd agree it was the right move for us at the time."

"Agreed," I smiled and sipped my coffee. "But I have a great business here. I'm doing my dream job of building a stadium. I can't just up and leave. You said that the distance would ruin our relationship..." We sat in silence for a few minutes.

"But we are at a different place. We are so much stronger. We can handle the distance now. My traveling first husband had cheated on me. This time, it would be me outside the house, and you know you can trust me."

"Wait, I'm not suggesting I don't. I'm worried about us, not anyone coming between us."

"Michael, I really want this job. It gets me right near the pinnacle of my career. We will talk on the phone every day. I'll visit you every weekend or you visit me. I'll tell you all the exciting things I'm doing, the assholes I meet, and the little men who think they can bully me that I'll have to straighten out. In a sense, we're both going on this new journey. No, not journey, adventure."

I was still hesitant, which she saw on my face.

"Look. I only need to do it for two years. Then, I'll get a superintendent job making four hundred thousand a year. We always say that we don't know anyone with a relationship like ours. We can survive this. I can kill it at this job, Michael."

"You can," I got up, helped her out of her chair, and hugged her. "And you will."

I was really happy for her as she hugged me tighter than ever. I silenced the nagging voice in my head that this would be a wrong move for us. In the end, though, I had to support her.

AUSTIN

Her daughter was going to Texas State University, near her job, so Jen stayed with her as she began her new career. Logan (my stepdaughter) lived an amazing life as a college student, and was ready for Mom to get her own place. Our deal with her was that she could experience college life and we'd pay all the bills so long as she passed her classes. We soon found a condo on Ladybird Lake in Downtown Austin and Jen was set. As Jen said, we talked on the phone daily and would visit each other on weekends. The weeks were lonely without my best friend there but the weekends were special, especially when I would go to Austin; it felt like mini-vacations.

I started to notice a slight shift in the beginning of 2019. Jen had her own place but would still meet with her daughter a couple times a week and come home tipsy. I wasn't used to a drunk or even tipsy Jen. We started getting into stupid little disagreements that I couldn't stop from turning into fights.

Then, inexplicably, her mother, who still stayed with me, started to mistreat me or talk badly about me while on the phone. Gone were the days of a grateful hello or a jovial conversation. Instead, I'd find myself close enough to overhear her talking to people on the speakerphone, "I don't know anymore. Jen is a consummate professional with a high position now. I don't like her with a construction guy. She should settle down with a doctor or lawyer."

Soon, the comments were made right at me under a teasing guise. I would quip back, "Don't forget, Mom, this construction worker retired your ass! I'd have to take a pay cut to make what many lawyers and doctors make." My home was no longer a peaceful haven.

The new house was nearly complete. But in an unforeseen turn of events, Jennifer's aunt, my mother-in-law's sister, moved in with us. I had built Jen and mine's new dream house, but Jen didn't live there! Yet, I had to put up with a salty mother-in-law and her wing-woman sister.

To top it off, Jen was going out 3 to 4 nights a week! It was what people call in polite society – "Bull Shit!"

I wasn't happy. I told Jen her mother and her aunt had to live with her. "I'm busting my ass over here coming home to an unhappy mother-in-law, I love her but she's your mom."

Her mother was pissed that she had to move to Austin, even though we got her a house at an Austin Country Club. Jen was still not home, but at least I got to come home to a tranquil environment, which I needed because, even though I was already a two-time Jiu-Jitsu Champion, I was training as hard as ever and building that stadium was taking a lot of my time.

Shortly after that, the every weekend visits started not to happen. "I'm sorry, hun, I have so much work to do this weekend."

"That's okay. I'll let you do your work. It's been two weeks."

Too many conversations started to end with her saying something like, "It's still not a good idea for this weekend. Next weekend, for sure!"

By month 16, it was evident that our marriage was struggling. I mulled about how to tell her for a week before I mentioned it. She had come home to visit for the weekend. We greeted each other with forced smiles and, for the first time, I was uncomfortable being in the same room with her. I had no idea how to start the conversation and assumed she didn't either. It was a Friday night when we had "The Talk."

THE TALK

"Jen, I know we made a plan for you to be there for two years, but these sixteen months have not gone according to plan. I need you to come back home. You don't need that job. You're amazing. You know I make plenty of money for both of us for you to take your time to find a great, fulfilling job here."

"But Michael, I love my job. I'm fulfilling my purpose."

"When we married, we said we'd always put each other first. Things aren't how we said they would be and you and me aren't how we were." I let the conversation hang in the air, nervous of where she would take it.

She let out a long sigh. "Michael, things aren't the way they were because everything has changed. I think we've grown apart."

"That's what I'm saying. We've grown apart. Come home and..."

"Michael," she interrupted. "I think we should get a divorce."

The impact didn't have as much as I thought it would if she ever told me those words because my initial reaction was that she was, in some way, joking. We talked long into the night and I remembered that she was not irrational or someone who didn't think twice before saying something important. She had been mulling over divorcing me for a while. Maybe it was that her mom was in her ear telling her she didn't need me.

"I thought we were a team?"

"I thought we had everything we wanted?"

"You were only going to be there for another seven months anyway."

We talked again about how to save the marriage. I would not bend, though, when it came to her mother. "We'll pay for your mom and aunt to live somewhere, but they can't live with me."

Ultimately, she said, "This is no longer working for me. I'm sorry Michael, but we've grown apart. We need a divorce."

She left the following day, Saturday, back to Austin. We talked a little bit, but it felt cold and distant. This was not my Jen. It wasn't long after when I got served divorce papers. I was devastated. Not even MMA fighters hit that hard.

Shortly before being served, there was a strange plague affecting millions worldwide and then billions. I got hit with divorce papers and then the world got hit with a global pandemic – COVID had arrived and was in full swing.

Not only was my marriage ending, but also all the lucrative projects I was working on were put on hold. Everything I had worked for was falling apart. The only person who I felt loved me for me, respected the person I was, and felt a lifelong connection to had abandoned me. I was in this big beautiful house all by myself. I didn't have work to keep my mind busy, I couldn't go to a gym to sweat out the misery, and I didn't have my best friend to talk to.

I'm not too proud to confess that my soul was hurting. I had no idea how deep and often the melancholy of sorrow could hit me. It was like being on the shore, getting hit by wave after wave after wave after wave of grief. As soon as I felt I'd be okay, the wave would hit me again. I have had breakups and gone to funerals for loved ones but had never felt torment like that before. I spent many nights wishing I could punch my frustrations away, only to eventually sleep on a pillow damp from tears shed in darkness. I would wake up to the hotness of pain and regret before getting out of bed. Everything I had worked for, everything I was proud of, was gone.

I looked at the bracelet on my wrist and started playing with it. I remembered being in prison and how I promised I'd make a life for myself. Slowly, instead of seeing the places where Jen and I would kiss in the house and feel remorse, I saw the house I had built and appreciated its art and creativity. I told myself, "Just keep doing what you're doing, Mike. Your conscience is clean. She'll realize what she did and come back or regret it."

When Javier gave me the bracelet, he said it was for the next time I was about to get in a fight, it would remind me I'm not the same person and get out of the fight. I don't think he ever imagined that the bracelet he gifted me helped me in the biggest fight of my life – against a me that wanted to quit on himself.

"You don't break, Mike. Fuck that!"

Jen and I talked about how to best part ways like adults. Luckily, she didn't intend to take me to the cleaners, which would have been beneath her character. She only wanted what she had earned, half of our cash and assets when I thought we were unbreakable. At the end, what we had once was strong enough to treat each other with dignity and we divided everything fairly. We agreed not to involve attorneys. In the great state of Texas, if there are no disagreements, a divorce can be done in as fast as 60 days, and for whatever reason, speed was her only concern. I NEVER want to know why. Our anniversary date was May 19; our divorce was final on July 22.

19

BLACK BELT MIKE

FIGHT TO WIN

GOING THROUGH AN EMOTIONAL DIVORCE IS ROUGH, BUT going through an emotional divorce during a pandemic that keeps you away from every other human being is a grueling, fucking nightmare. Jen had permanently moved out and loneliness had moved in. There weren't even any sports on TV to keep my mind off my now ex-wife. Of course, COVID-19 brought many other problems. Some of my customers told me they couldn't pay their invoices!

The problem was my guys had already performed the work, they expected and deserved to be paid! One outstanding invoice that didn't get paid was for $190K! My integrity fought with my desire to keep my lifestyle, but in the end, integrity won and I paid all my employees and most of my subcontractors. However, I could only pay some of them all they were owed. It's a terrible feeling to tell good, hard-working people that you don't have their money but that was where Covid brought me and many other employers in many verticals. I was at a new all-time low.

Around this time, my buddy Seth Daniels called me. He was a Jiu-Jitsu Superfight promoter. He is a well-known figure in the jiu-jitsu community and we had become quite close. At this point I had retired from competing, but always worked his shows when he came to Dallas. At one point, I was the #1 ranked light heavyweight in the country for F2W. I never had a boring match. After the ways guys express pleasantries, he told me the reason for his call.

"So, listen, the fucking world is shut down, but you know I'm not gonna just sit around and wait. Dallas is the only place I can do shows. We can't have an audience so we'll stream it live. The problem is, Team No Sleep needs to travel with me to make this shit happen. I don't have to tell you how tight money is for a promoter these days. I was wondering, is there any way we can stay with you? Mostly just the team and occasionally a fighter or two if needed."

I didn't know if this was an answered prayer or if things were about to get worse. I've always been mindful of who I call a friend and what a friend is, and I considered Seth a friend, so I rolled the dice with him.

"Well, I'm the only one in a pretty big house. You all can stay but there are rules. I'm not a frat boy, so this ain't a frat house. I don't want to live in a party house. If everyone can abide by the rules, sure man."

"Awesome, Mike, you're really helping a brother out!"

"It's all good," I smiled. "Mi casa, su casa."

Seth and Team No Sleep came to my house and stayed with me all summer. The entire vibe of the place had changed from a sad, woe-is-me vibe to a bunch of athletes joking around, cooking, doing a little wrestling, and being guys. I still had my boat, and, being that the government couldn't shut the lake down, I was there every weekend. On fight nights, I was the head referee.

One night, I was at a Rules Meeting before the event and Seth sent a message to come to the booth. I got there and he looked a little worried but also as if he was suppressing a grin.

"Mike, I need a favor. As you know, you have to have a negative Covid test to be here. Well, my two commentators drove together and on the way here, one got the results that he tested positive."

"Oh shit," I mumbled.

"And what's worse, the one that tested negative can't come either because he was driving with the one that was positive!"

"Shit, Seth, what are you gonna do?"

Seth let out the smirk. "I need you to do commentary tonight."

"What? I never did that! Besides, I'm the ref."

"Trust me, commenters are a lot harder to find than refs. You know all there is to know about this sport. You speak well enough. Please tell me you'll fucking do it. You'll be fine."

"Well, I'll try it. Don't get mad at me if I suck though."

In what seemed like a blur, I had sheets of notes from the competitors in front of me, lights in my face, and a headset on. Once the show began, I started saying shit I thought I was supposed to.

"Good evening, everyone; this is Black Belt Mike and welcome to Fight 2 Win!" I didn't put too much pressure on myself. I figured, "Fuck it, have fun!" I knew what I was talking about and knew most of the men and women on the card. My commentary came so fast and present with the action, it looked like I had seen the fights before!

About halfway through the show, Seth told me I was their new commentator. With no training or preparation, I became the voice of the Fight 2 Win promotion!

Sports fans were hungry to watch any competition during Covid, so with MMA and Jiu Jitsu tournaments probably the only live sports on TV, we became pretty popular, at least regionally, and I became pretty well known in that community. I thought it humbling but cool as hell that people started to notice me and ask, "Hey, Black Belt Mike, can I have a picture with you?" The funniest times were when people would hear my voice and say, "You almost sound like Black Belt Mike!"

UFC FIGHT PASS

After commentating on approximately twenty shows, my good friend of many years, Stephen Tecci, reached out to me. He had a degree in Finance from Tulane but had spent most of his adult life as a rock star. He was working for the UFC in a Finance role (and later became a VP of Research, OTT, and digital transnational business growth for PPV and UFC Fight Pass.) We caught up quickly, as good friends do, and he asked, "I heard you're doing commentary on Flo for F2W. How's that going?"

I told him I was having fun with it but wasn't about to quit my day job. He laughed and said he would listen in on that night's show. After the show, he called to congratulate me but also said, "If you work on a few things, I might be able to get you in with the UFC on Fight Pass."

I didn't take it too seriously but took his criticism seriously and worked on improving on everything he had mentioned. I continued to do the F2W shows when they came to the Dallas area. But, as Covid continued its rampage, all the work I could still do got postponed indefinitely. I was left with no jobs and nothing to do again.

I put some feelers out and a friend I had worked with on Globe Life Stadium was now the COO for an Electrical Contractor. He asked if I could help get his business operations in order. This was a big company, grossing upwards of $200M in volume per year – and they were growing. I started as their first GS (General Superintendent) but got promoted to Director of Field Operations before long. In what seemed pretty sudden, I was overseeing more than 1200 employees with a fleet of more than 100 vehicles, a large warehouse full of inventory, and general and heavy equipment totaling more than $20 M in equipment. They were all under my supervision, meaning my responsibility. However, it was up my alley, and knew I could shine in that role in a company like that. Shortly after settling into my new role, I got another call from Tecci.

"What are you doing this weekend?"

"Maybe just fucking around on the lake again, why? What's up?"

We have an event this weekend in Houston. Wear a suit and plan on staying until Monday."

I hung up the phone excitedly. I looked in my closet and saw the three thousand dollar suit I had only worn twice. "Oh ya, come to me, you beautiful mother fucker!"

I showed up dressed to the nines, complete with a Media Pass that Tecci had given me. Tecci proceeded to introduce me to some of the top people that were there.

On Saturday night, we went to the UFC Pay-Per-View at the Toyota Center and then the Fury FC show on Sunday night. They were taping the "Dana White: Looking For A Fight" Series and said we'd be guests.

He introduced me to Eric Garcia, the promoter/owner of Fury Fighting Championships. "Tecci says you're a good commentator. Can you do a show with me next weekend here in Houston? Our regular guy just took a job with ESPN."

"Um, ya. I'd be honored." *I was going to replace a professional broadcaster now working for ESPN. Shit. Was I ready for this?*

"Great. It'll be you, UFC welterweight Alex Morono and Todd Moore. You'll do the color."

Later, Tecci told me, "Congrats, man, but, so you know, we're not paying you for the event next weekend. Also, because people know we're good friends, I will be extra critical of you so people can't say the UFC plays favorites. If you blow it, you blow it."

I shook his hand and thanked him.

"Look down," he smiled, "your foot is in the door."

Then, we celebrated with many laughs and drinks. I made the trip back to Dallas Fort Worth the next day with a smile, knowing I had some work to do.

The first chance I got, I Googled what the hell a color commentator did. I was a one-man show at Fight 2 Win, unless my brother, Bobby "Beast-

Mode" Alexander showed up, but I had never worked in a 3-man team. I felt like a "Minor League Joe Rogan."

My primary duty was to assist the play-by-play commentator. With three people talking, I had to decide the right time to give my "expert opinion" without talking over the other two commentators. I prepared by watching other fights and focused on the three-man weave as commentators danced around each other and gave the fight a voice.

I did my first show for Fury Fighting Championships on UFC Fight Pass in June of 2021.

Afterward, Tecci called me. "You killed it. Welcome to UFC Fight Pass and Fury Fighting Championship!"

20

PERSONAL RESPONSIBILITY

FUCK THE STATS

I HOPE MY STORY HAS ENTERTAINED YOU AND PROVED A good use of your valuable time. As you've read, I've had my highs – excellent career success, a two-time Jiu Jitsu World Champion, and a voice for UFC Fight Pass – and I've had my lows – an abused child, years in prison, and being divorced are only a few of them. I shared all of this with you in an attempt to inspire you to never quit on your dreams, even if you're not sure what they are just yet.

I will humbly admit that I am lucky and blessed to live the life I do – although I also acknowledge the amount of work I had to do to get here. Allow me to pass on some of what I've learned along the way...

First and foremost, get rid of EVERYONE who doesn't support your goals. That goes for loved family members and childhood friends, too. I don't care how popular one thinks they might be, no one has 100 or more real friends. If you believe it, you're lying to yourself. If something devastating happened to you, like going to jail, see how many

GET RID OF EVERYONE WHO DOESN'T SUPPORT YOUR GOALS.

would believe you, write you, check on you, send you money, check to make sure your kids are being well fed, or defend you when others talk bad about you when you're not around. You'll be amazed to discover that you may have two or three people who truly support you and your goals.

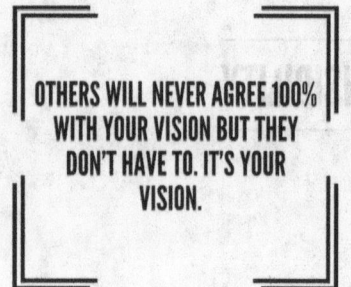

OTHERS WILL NEVER AGREE 100% WITH YOUR VISION BUT THEY DON'T HAVE TO. IT'S YOUR VISION.

The thing is, most people don't know their crabs. Have you ever seen a bucket filled with crabs? As soon as one of them seems to figure out how to get out of the bucket, another crab holds on to it and keeps it in the bucket! Others will never agree 100% with your vision but they don't have to. It's YOUR vision. They'll come from a place of love and wanting to protect you from yourself and try to talk you out of starting a business or reaching for the stars.

"What do you know about running a business?"

The truth is, they are too fearful to live out loud and, without even knowing it or doing it consciously, project their fears onto others trying to make big moves.

We are supposed to outgrow certain people. Sure, it's great to have friends for 30, 40, or 50 years – but if they don't support your goal, let them be friends from far. They no longer belong in your inner circle. However, when you outgrow them and don't talk to them anymore, it'll be okay because you will have found others who walk, talk, think, and strive like you.

By all accounts, I should not have lived the life I have in the last 15 years. My good friend, Dr. Gino Collura, told me that based on my past, he would have given me a .01% chance that I would be successful, with the other 99.9% predicting that I would have landed back in jail or winded up broke or would be dead by now.

I get it. I came from ugly. I was an abused child. My mother was a drug addict that tried to end my life, twice! I was a disgruntled teen who moved into a new high school and never quite fit in. I had severe anger issues, which ultimately led me to spend years of my life in jail. Every statistic on recidivism would tell you that I was bound to go back to prison based on my history. I have something to say about that – fuck those stats. Stats don't determine who I became and stats sure as hell shouldn't define who you become.

The changing point in my life was when I took a long, serious look at myself and realized I didn't like the person I was. I hated the environment I had put myself in. Once I stopped blaming others for MY SITUATION and decided to take PERSONAL RESPONSIBILITY for the rest of my life, things slowly changed for the better.

YOU HAVE TO SUFFER TO GET BETTER

It's so sad, but most people live their one and only life not even liking it! They dread waking up and getting out of bed to face the day. Some need to make fun of others to feel better about themselves, while others need to be high or drunk to escape their cowardice and pass out. Most people live lives they don't like because they believe they don't have the fortitude to change. Here's a truth bomb for you that you might not like: You have to suffer to get better. Practicing self-restraint when you've given in to your cravings for decades is difficult. Living a life of instant gratification will not bring you to your dream life.

Many people might consider me successful, and if making more than a million dollars in one year and becoming a world champion is what others think success, I'll take it, although I know many people a lot further ahead than me. All I know is that I don't rest on any laurels and continue working to live the life I dream for myself.

I hope, dear reader, you're also on the same journey. Be careful of the pitfalls toward success. Every time you improve your position, someone might notice. You might get an atta-boy, atta-girl, a positive comment on social media, or a physical pat on the back. Be mindful that although that feels good, you haven't reached your goal yet. Too many people are resting on their success journey because they're fat and happy with just receiving acknowledgments. They're fooling themselves. They're not resting, they've landed and now they're stuck.

It's good to know people notice the hard work you're doing, it's the first indicator that you're on the right track. Use it to become more determined, but not to feel like you're already there.

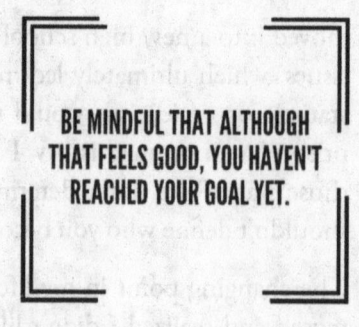

BE MINDFUL THAT ALTHOUGH THAT FEELS GOOD, YOU HAVEN'T REACHED YOUR GOAL YET.

Do a personal assessment like I did. Find out what you're good at. Make a list of things you think you want to accomplish. Then, cross out the ones that didn't come from your heart, the ones that other people think you should do. Double down on the things you're good at. I would have never been a Jiu Jitsu World Champion if I didn't stop focusing on striking and doubled down on Jits. Get better at what you're good at. Then, become the best in your circle, industry, family, or community. Become an asset, not a liability.

IT TAKES PATIENCE TO WIN

Here's another truth bomb for you: It takes patience to win the game of life. I got out of jail and took a job with my father laying rock under the merciless Texas sun for a whopping twelve dollars an hour. After work, I'd shower and go work out. I didn't have the time or the money to take a girl out. I did a complete 360 on what my life was like before going to prison. I stuck with it. I didn't go partying once I got a little bit of money. I couldn't if I wanted to keep the promise I made to myself that I'd be more intelligent and more patient.

REPETITION WORKS

Truth bomb # 3: Repetition works. I remember starting Jiu Jitsu, a strong 200-pound man getting beat by a 140-pound woman! It was humbling, to say the least. But I showed up the next day, and the next, and the next. Understand that just like failing is repeatable, so is success.

Your trajectory might go straight up for a while; whatever you do, don't change the recipe. You are creating massive momentum that will help you when you inevitably start going up and down. In other words, keep your eye on the prize, not what you can afford at the moment.

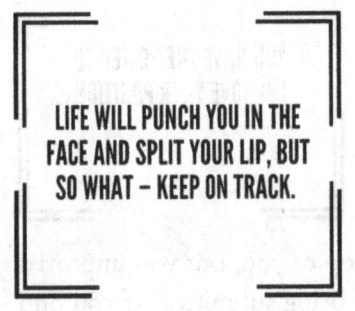

LIFE WILL PUNCH YOU IN THE FACE AND SPLIT YOUR LIP, BUT SO WHAT – KEEP ON TRACK.

I would have never had a million dollars in my savings account if I continued to spend money like I did before. I had to change and be patient with rewarding myself. Life will punch you in the face and split your lip, but so what – keep on track. Too many people try to convince others with their sad stories about why they're not ahead in life instead of talking to those who are where they wish to be to find out how that person got there.

If you had a rough childhood, does it matter still? A holocaust survivor wrote a book called Undaunted. Her sister was shot in the head while standing next to her. Her mother and twin little sisters were carted off to the gas chambers. She was beaten, forced to take electrical shock therapy, and stripped of every human dignity. THAT is a rough childhood. But you know what she did when she got free? She came to America and DECIDED to have a wonderful life. She didn't take any medication or see any psychiatrists. She passed away peacefully in her 90s, leaving the home she owned, her three sons, twelve grandchildren, and 21 great-grandchildren. At her funeral, more than one person said she was the life of the party. You can stop it with the pity party, you're the only one there.

YOUR PAST DOESN'T MATTER, ONLY YOUR FUTURE

My point in telling you her story is that your past doesn't matter. Stop dwelling on it and get with living your life. Let go of that woe-is-me medicine that keeps you mired in mediocrity. If you have to talk to a psychiatrist, do it! You're losing the game of life! Wake up!

I leave you with this challenge – be better. Say it daily – "I'm going to be better today." Then, keep the promises you make to yourself.

No matter where you find yourself, you have the power to improve your position. In Jiu-Jitsu, you rarely win a fight with one move. Usually, it takes minutes of testing your strength against your opponent. He or she may get you in a bad spot, but all you have to do is one move to improve your

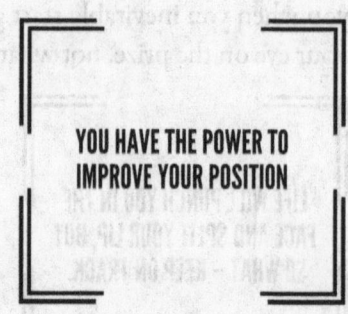

YOU HAVE THE POWER TO IMPROVE YOUR POSITION

position. Your opponent may still be on top of you, but you improved your position and are no longer at risk of being submitted. If you find yourself in a dominant spot, improve your position until you get to where you can apply a fight-ending submission.

Do the same with life. Improve your position and live a better life, the life your children deserve, and leave a legacy that would have made your ancestors proud.

21

THROUGH THE YEARS

5 or 6 years old. Look at all that hair!

Springtown High School Varsity track as a freshman. Buff!

US Nave Boot Camp, Great Lakes Illinois 1994

Playing slot receiver for the Fort Worth Texans at 25 years old.

My first MMA picture a few weeks before my first fight. I put tape of the UFC logo so no one would think I was being a poser!

TJ Desantis, Pearl Gonzalez, and myself doing cometary for the inaugural UFC Fight Pass Invitational at the UFC Apex in Las Vegas. Dec 2021

Hosting the bracket reveal at the ADCC World Championship in Las Vegas. Sept 2022. Left to right - Gordon Ryan, me, Mo Jassim, Andre Galvao. Photo credit:@kyushotya Kye Lee

*Michael and Shannon at a photo shoot! Suit by @qclother. Photo credit
@marynamphotography*

Interviewing Themba Gorimbo after his final fight for Fury Fighting Championshihps before being signed to the UFC. Pho Credit - Mike "The Truth" Jackson

With the Tecci brothers. Left to right: Stephen, Me, Paul, and Mike Tecci before a UFC fight in Dallas.

Winning quarter finals match at the Inaugural ADCC Open in Las Vegas in September of 2022. I came out of retirement and got the Bronze! Photo credit: Jordan Huynh @jordanhfoto

ABOUT THE AUTHOR

Michael Ray Alexander was born to Lawrence and Patricia Alexander at Tripler Army Medical Center in Waipahu, Hawaii. He is the second-oldest of his siblings – older brother Jason, sister Joni, and little brother Coty. His parents separated and his mother moved him and his siblings to Fort Worth, Texas when he was two. Today, he resides in Godley, Texas.

From humble beginnings, he became a football and track star in high school. After high school, he decided to serve our country, joined the Navy, and attended Yeoman A School. After a stint in prison, he started his construction business and has been in many high-level executive roles ever since.

AS A COMPETITOR:

After medical reasons cut his MMA career short, he focused on Jiu-Jitsu. He won his first Brazilian Jiu-Jitsu World Championship in 2013. He won his second World Championship in 2014.

AS AN EXECUTIVE IN CONSTRUCTION:

He was intricately involved in the Globe Life Field Stadium (Texas Rangers Stadium), a billion-dollar project.

PERSONALLY:

After coming close several times, Mike made a million dollars in a single year for the 1st time in the 2019 calendar year.

AS A COMMENTATOR:

Michael Alexander, also known as Black Belt Mike, commentated for Fight2Win before getting signed by Fury Fighting Championships as a color commentator on UFC Fight Pass, and Commentated the Inaugural UFC Fight Pass Invitational at the UFC Apex. Two of his ring interviews are the most watched interviews on the UFC FP social media.

AT THE TIME OF THIS WRITING:

Mike has commentated on more than 40 shows on UFC Fight Pass and is an executive for a construction company. However, his passion for speaking and helping people also has him speaking on various topics, including defeating childhood trauma, construction operations, having a Winner's Mindset, improving in Jiu-Jitsu, and many others.

To book Michael Alexander to speak at your event, email him directly at Mike@blackbeltmike.com.

ACKNOWLEDGMENTS

First and foremost I'd like to thank my immediate family: Thanks for putting up with me early in life and then supporting me during the worst times. Thank God I finally recognized the gifts I was blessed with and doubled down on them. I thank God every day for sparing me early in my life. Thanks to your love and support when I needed it most, I will leave the world better than I found it.

Dr. J, Logan and Chase: Thank you for supporting me and teaching me that unconditional love does exist. Helping your mother raise you is possibly my favorite accomplishment and I am so proud of the adults you are. No matter how much time passes, you can always call if you ever need anything or just want to talk. I will always love you and will never forget what we had.

My father Lawrence Alexander: Thanks for taking me from the hell I was living in and trying your best to make our home functional for me and my siblings. The last five years of your life I was so proud of our relationship and I will never forget the talk we had on our drive 2 weeks before you passed. I'm taking care of mom.

Darla Alexander, my real mother although the world would call you my step mom: I was a wild 7 yr. old when we met and you were only 19. (My dad was 29, what a perv lol) You stayed around and raised us and was with my father until the day he died. You are the only mother I will ever claim and I thank you so much for treating Jason, Joni and myself as your own. We love you so much. I will always take care of you, as promised.

Jason, my oldest brother: Thank you for saving my life when I was 5. You were such a good, compliant kid. It's hard to believe you did that for me. I wasn't always nice to you, but I love you and I have your back. Thank you for buying me shoes when I had nothing. I knew you couldn't afford them, but you still did it. I was so happy to be able to pay you back the way I did many years later.

Joni, my sister: You have a beautiful presence and an infectious laugh. Never change that. I never had kids so it was my honor to help you raise Jake and Tyler. I love you and the boys with all of my heart.

Coty, my little brother: You have such a kind heart and wear it visibly on your sleeve. I hope you find your way and just know you have my support. I am so sorry I wasn't a better role model early in life. But I love you so much. Thank you for blessing me with my niece Lainie. She is all of the best parts of you magnified.

The Tecci's: Paul, Stephen and Mike: We met when I was 10 yrs. old and quickly became close with all of you. Thank you for your lifelong friendship and picking up right where we left off no matter how long it's been. Who would have thought our paths would have crossed again the way they did. I tell everyone, the Tecci boys are all brilliant. I hope I bring half the value to your life that you have brought to mine.

Rudy, my high school friend: You recognized the change in me immediately when it started to happen. Thank you for coming back around and taking our friendship for what it was. I'm happy to see you thriving and still coaching football and I appreciate seeing you on our text thread saying "Finally."

Leon, my high school friend: I've never told you how much I envied your work ethic and the kind of man you have always been. Very similar backgrounds, but you always took the high road. From sweeping those floors to running that entire company and everything in between, I've always admired the way you handled your business. Thank you for always having my back and being the voice of reason, even as teenagers.

Gary Rushing, My high school football and track coach: When everyone was wondering why this kid was acting out, but never cared to ask, you did. You always took up for me and made me believe I had a greater purpose. You were never easy on me and always got the most out of me. At that time of my life I was terrified of disappointing you. I failed I'm sure at that point in my life. Thank you for talking me into staying and finishing there. You have made a lifelong impact on my life and I will never forget. Looking forward to that dinner.

Jimmy Sullivan, my roommate while in the Navy: Thanks for big brothering me while I was learning how to be an adult. Thanks for letting me use your ID to get into Coasties. And thank you for our continued friendship. It's been too long. And Texas is a beautiful place to retire. Think about it.

Jennifer E, known as Sheila in this book: I am so happy that we have found each other and established a friendship at this point in our lives. I was a terrible husband at that point in my life, and for that I am sorry. Thank you for seeing the good in me and being there anytime I want to talk. I value our friendship and always look forward to making you laugh uncontrollably. Always makes my day.

Javier Ontiveros, my friend and guard at the prison: Thank you for talking to me like a normal human when other COs talked to us like we were trash. You are a big reason I started to explore myself and why I kept failing. You made the time bearable just by treating me as a friend and not a convict. I will never forget everything you did for me and I am grateful for your continued friendship.

Brad Imes, Former Teammate and TUF Season 2 alum: At the busiest time of your life you always found time to write and send pictures. And then had me set up to train once I got out. You have no idea how much the letters and pictures helped pass the time and motivated me to be ready for what I would be doing once I got home. I'm so happy to see you living your best life with such a beautiful family.

Debra Goodman-Miller: I love you so much. Then, and now. You have been my friend through everything. You wrote me, supported me and kept me sane at times when I thought I'd go crazy. I cannot tell you how happy it makes me to see how you are with your boys. I will do anything for you and will always be a phone call away. Thank you for being a great friend to me.

Travis Lutter, my Jiu Jitsu/MMA Coach: This is a tough one to write because I still have no idea what caused the change of heart. But regardless, the almost 10 years I spent learning from you are some of my best and favorite memories as I was rebuilding my life. You and your family were as important in my life as anything at one point. I am grateful for the time I spent at Team Lutter and still have great friends there. I still consider earning my black belt from Travis as one of my greatest accomplishments. It makes me happy to see your school, your kids, and your legacy continuing to grow.

Ricardo Liborio, Brazilian Jiu Jitsu Legend: Thank you for letting me train and visit you at ATT when you had no business letting this blue belt amateur MMA fighter in with all of those savages. You treated me as any other student and put me right in there with all of the big timers. Every time I've seen you since then you always have kind words and make time to talk. I am grateful for our friendship and always look forward to running into you. You are what I aspire to be to future generations in Jiu Jitsu and MMA.

Albert Hughes and Genesis Jiu Jitsu: Thank you so much for taking me in and giving me a home gym and a competitive atmosphere to continue my journey in Jiu Jitsu. www.genesisjiujitsu.com

Dr. Gino Collura: One of the best decisions I made was sending that message that day. As I told you my story you immediately invited me into your life as someone you believed you could help. Every time we talk I learn something. This book would have never happened if it weren't for you. Thank you for freeing me from my fear of the past and making me realize that my story might help others. I am forever in your debt.

Seth Daniels: You have a knack for calling or texting me at the perfect time. From F2W Pro 6 when I first competed for you and blew the roof off that place with my match against Rocki to the time when I needed company most during Covid and my divorce. You continue to pop up in the most significant moments in my life and add to them. Thank you for being there. Thank you for putting me behind the mic. Thank you for introducing me to the entire Jiu Jitsu community. I wish everyone knew the Seth Daniels that only a handful of people and me know. Your boys are very lucky to have you as a father. I've got your back.

Mo Jassim: During the biggest show in the history of the sport you found a place to work me onto the camera and be part of the greatest grappling event in history. Thank you for the hospitality you've always showed from my visit to Puerto Rico, to ADCC in Las Vegas, and beyond. I appreciate you and all you are doing for the Jiu Jitsu community and I am thankful for our friendship.

Eric Garcia and Richard Burmaster: I can't say enough how much I appreciate you guys giving me the opportunity to call fights for Fury Fighting Championships and allowing me to grow into the position. I hope you feel that I have given you everything you expected and more. It is important to me to represent the promotion the way it deserves. You are the best and I look forward to doing this until I'm too ugly to be on camera.

TJ DeSantis, AJ Hoffman and Todd Moore: At the time of this writing, I have done 40 events on UFC Fight Pass. As a guy who was just a former fighter and jiu-jitsu guy, working with each one of you was an important learning experience and I appreciate each of you for those lessons. I hope to get to work with each of you again. Thanks again for your patience when working with this amateur.

Raheel Ramzanali and Alex Morono: The magic made each event is one of the highlights of my life. I am so thankful for you guys and always look forward to calling fights, shooting the shit and getting a few rounds in with Alex the day before. You guys are very important to me and I hope I bring as much fun to your lives as you bring to mine.

Shannon O'Shea. When we met finally, I knew that you were someone I needed in my life. And now 2 years later I'm so happy for the path we are on. I love you so much and love the way you love me. It makes me so happy and I look forward to seeing what's next. I love you!!

Jason House, Thank you so much for helping me navigate my way through this industry and always looking out for me. Thank you for your friendship. I am so happy to be part of the Iridium family.

The Jiu Jitsu/MMA Community-Thank you so much for accepting me and making me feel welcome anywhere I go in the world. I will continue to try to give back what this community has given me. I love you all and wish you all happy and healthy lives.

The UFC: Thank you for letting me be a small part of the family. Sean Shelby, thank you for your friendship and always having my back. Stephen Tecci, thank you for the opportunity and cutting me no slack. I am so grateful to be part of this mega family.

Eli Gonzalez: You're an amazing ghostwriter! I am so grateful to have the Godfather of Ghostwriting to help me tell this story. Thank you so much for pulling me through this process and sharing your story with me as well. I'm also proud that you and your team published this book. You have a friend in Texas for life. I hope my gratitude showed through this process. I am forever grateful. GO COWBOYS!

Motive Actual: Thank you for connecting with me and sharing the passion for Improving Your Position! I love to support small businesses, especially when great people run them. Get your Improve Your Position T-shirt at www.motiveactual.com

Chris Crail and Cauliflower Nation: Thank you for your friendship and asking for my input for your apparel. Mostly, anytime I needed a walkout shirt, brand ideas, or anything else, you were always game. I really appreciate you and always look forward to catching up. www.cauliflowernation.com

Mike Smith, Vice President of Con Real: I can't thank you enough for introducing me to the business side of our industry, which can also be the ugly side. I am forever grateful for your leadership and happy to have you as one of my mentors. I've always got your back.

Chris Martinez, Owner/CEO Phalanx Apparel: It's rare to buy a product that you love over and over and then end up with such a great relationship to that product and it's founder. Thank you for supporting me in my final years of competing and becoming a friend. I love it when we bounce ideas off each other and I love supporting Phalanx, the best No Gi apparel in the sport. The storms we experience always end with sunshine. Thank you Chris. I am always a phone call away. www. phalanxfc.com

Vandal Kimonos: Thank you Kiah for making an indestructible Gi. I'm so happy I found you. I now have probably 25 Gi's from Vandal Kimonos and that just might last me a lifetime! Get one at www. vandalkimonos.com

Corby Dodson: Thank you for everything you've done for me and continue to do today. You have always had my back and I feel extremely lucky to be in a position to make sure I have yours. The world needs more people like you.

www.ingramcontent.com/pod-product-compliance
Lightning Source LLC
Chambersburg PA
CBHW011229120626
46549CB00008B/3201